THE EMPEROR JULIAN.

THE EMPEROR JULIAN

AND

HIS GENERATION.

AN HISTORICAL PICTURE,

BY

AUGUSTUS NEANDER, D. D.,

PROFESSOR OF DIVINITY IN THE UNIVERSITY OF BERLIN.

TRANSLATED BY

G. V. COX, M. A.,

ESQUIRE BEDELL IN THE UNIVERSITY OF OXFORD.

Ἄνθρωπος παντόπορος ἄπορος.—SOPHOC.
Σὺ δὲ θαρσεῦ, ἐπεὶ θεῖον γενὸς ἐστὶ βρότοισι.

Wipf and Stock Publishers
150 West Broadway • Eugene OR 97401
2001

The Emperor Julian and His Generation

By Neander, Augustus and Cox, G.V.
ISBN: 1-57910-751-6

Reprinted by *Wipf and Stock Publishers*
150 West Broadway • Eugene OR 97401

Previously published by J.C. Riker 1850.

CONTENTS.

TRANSLATOR'S PREFACE.

THE history of Julian, at all times striking, has been lately brought into revived notice. Public attention has been invited to his name in more than one recent publication. Strauss has made use of Julian's character as a vehicle for an elaborate *jeu-d'esprit* against the King of Prussia. (See the *Edinburgh Review* for July, 1848.) And Macaulay, in his *History of England*, vol. ii. p. 104, has given us an earlier specimen of that sort of wit, in a learned parallel between Julian and James II., by a priest of the Church of England named Johnson.

It cannot then be unseasonable to present to the public, in an English dress, Dr. Neander's monograph, which was first recommended to my notice by Niebuhr's praise. (See his *Correspondence*, vol. ii. p. 161.)

This little work was published as long ago as 1812, and much of it has since been incorporated in Neander's *General History of the Christian Religion and Church*. The reader will see for himself that though the writer does justice to the ambitious grandeur of

Julian's enterprise (to restore the Old Worship), he does not praise it, but rather accounts for its short-lived success from the character of the age as well as the qualities of the man. He may write *con amore* of the hero of his book, his love of learning, his courage, his moral purity, &c., but he is not to be classed (as in the *Edinburgh Review*) among his "warmest defenders," except against contemporaneous calumnies and subsequent exaggerations. The impiety and folly of his attempt, his vanity and long-practised hypocrisy, are nowhere more strongly delineated. To me he has always been, and still is, "Julian the Apostate;" and notwithstanding the toleration he professed, his short reign was long enough to show that he was in a fair way to become Julian the Persecutor. I will only add one hint to the English reader, who, thanks to the soundness of our Theology, may look with suspicion upon even the best of German Theologians; this hint is suggested by the title of the Work, viz., that the spirit of Julian's age, rather than the history of Julian himself, is the real subject of the book here translated.

Instead therefore of any farther remarks of my own, I will give the reader a specimen of the mode in which Julian's character has been handled by a distinguished Theologian of our own Church, Bishop Warburton, whose writings are now more celebrated than read. It is scarcely necessary to refer to Gibbon whose account of Julian (vol. iv. ch. 23, 4), with the usual allowance for sneers and sarcasm, is on the whole tolerably fair.

To the extract from Warburton, I prefix, in lieu of a portrait, a graphic delineation of Julian by his cotemporary, Gregory Nazianzen (which I translate from Professor Ullmann's *Life of Gregory*), together with a few touches from his own pencil and that of Ammianus.

Extract translated from PROFESSOR ULLMANN'S "*Life of Gregory Nazianzen,*" p. 36.

At Athens, Gregory formed an acquaintance (of a very remarkable character, and one which subsequently gave him no pleasure) with the nephew of the Emperor Constantius, the prince *Julian*, who afterwards succeeded to the throne, and played a short but extraordinary part in the drama of the world's history. This prince was then (A. D. 355) resident there, by the permission of his jealous uncle, for the purpose of pursuing his studies. A singular predilection for paganism and pagan mysteries, which flourished particularly in that city, already displayed itself in Julian. He was as strongly attracted to the rhetorical and philosophical advocates of heathenism, as they in their turn (as well as all the admirers of the old religion) directed their attention, with hopeful expectation, to the young and distinguished member of the imperial family. Gregory, therefore, who acknowledges that he by no means possessed a quick-sightedness in discerning character, had yet no difficulty even then in anticipating the very worst in Julian. He calls upon those who were with him at that time at Athens, to testify that soon after he had become acquainted with Julian, he had uttered those words, "How great an evil is the Roman empire here training up!"* What it was which caused Gregory to judge so severely of the young man,† he has himself informed us, in a perhaps somewhat exaggerated picture of Julian's demeanor and external appearance: "I was led to become a prophet‡ (he says) by the restlessness of his behavior, and the exaggerated tone of his animation. It also appeared to me to be no good sign, that his neck was not strongly set on his shoulders; that those shoulders often moved convulsively; that his eye frequently glanced round timidly and rolled as if in phrenzy; and that his feet were never in a state of repose. As little was I pleased with his nose, which breathed pride and contempt; with the ridiculous distortions of his face, which yet indicated the same pride; his loud, immoderate laughter; the nodding and shaking of his head without any reason; his hesitating speech, interrupted by the act of breathing; his abrupt, unmeaning questions, and his answers not at all better, but often self-contradictory, and given without any scientific arrangement."§ If we allow for that which gave to the pen of

* Οἶον κακὸν ἡ 'Ρωμαίων τρέφει.

† His junior only by six years.

‡ See Gregory's *Orat.* v. 23 and 24, pp. 161, 2.

§ It is not uninteresting to compare with the above what Julian himself tells us of his own external appearance. He evidently tried much, especially as Emperor, to keep up a peculiar exhibition of himself, and was fond of uniting the unpolished severity of a Cynic with the dignified bearing of an ancient hero. With self-satisfied complacency he speaks (in his *Misopogon*, p. 338, seq.) of his bristly hair, his manly breast, and his long, shaggy beard, while he still censures Nature for not having given him a handsomer countenance. Nay, he does not hesitate to speak in terms of commendation of his ink-stained hands, his long nails, and even of the minute inhabitants which dwelt in the wilderness of his beard!

Ammianus, Marcellinus (xxv. 4) gives a much more agreeable description of him than he does of himself: "Mediocris erat staturæ, capillis, tanquam pexisset, mollibus, hirsuta barba in acutum desinente vestitus, venustate oculorum micantium flagrans, qui mentis ejus angustias indicabant, superciliis decoris et naso rectissimo, ore paullo majore, labro this delineator so powerful an aversion, we have still remaining the picture of a restless, fiery-tempered man, of a mind incessantly active and excited; of one who was haughty in the conscious feeling of power, but yet externally practising dissimulation; while there was wanting to his great natural abilities that suitable education which would have regulated and directed them to a right object.

Extract from BISHOP WARBURTON'S "*Julian.*"
(Quarto Edition of his Works, vol. iv. p. 374.)

There was a time when the *powers of this world* were all opposed to the progress of the *Gospel*. The first attempt upon Christianity was such as was most natural to this *power*, the suppressing it by brutal force; and the subjection of the whole civilized world to the despotic will of one blind persecutor gave that force its utmost moment. But this method of attack required a comprehensive knowledge of human nature, and of the doctrines to be suppressed.

Few of the persecuting emperors had either. M. Antoninus had the one; Julian only, who closed the scene, had both. Till his time the sole engine was simple force. Julian was the first who got enough acquainted with the Gospel to apply such arms against it as must have ended in its ruin, had it been nothing more than what he affected to think it, a human invention. And here we shall be forced to confess, that Providence seems to have raised up this extraordi-

inferiore demisso, opima et incurva cervice, humeris vastis et latis, ab ipso capite usque unguium summitates lineamentorum recta compage, unde viribus valebat et cursu."—In another passage Ammianus mentions some peculiarities which agree better with Gregory's description: "Levioris ingenii,..........linguæ fusioris et admodum raro silentis."

N. B. Ullmann here, and even Neander in his history, speak of Julian as *nephew* instead of *cousin* to Constantius, as Gibbon and Warburton describe him. Julian's father, called Julius Constantius, was brother to Constantine, and uncle to Constantius the Emperor, who being Constantine's son, was therefore Julian's cousin.

nary man on set purpose to do the last honors to the religion of Jesus; to show the world what *human power*, with all its advantages united, was able to oppose to its establishment. For we find in this emperor all the great qualities that a projector could conceive, or an adversary would require, to secure success to so daring an opposition. He was eloquent and liberal; artful, insinuating, and indefatigable; which, joined to a severe temperance, an affected love of justice, and a courage superior to all trials, first gained him the affections, and, soon after, the peaceable possession of the whole empire.

He was bred up in the Christian religion from his infancy: and was obliged to profess it (or at least to disguise his passion for paganism) to the time he assumed the purple.* His aversion to his uncle Constantine and his cousin Constantius, for the cruelties exercised on his family, had prejudiced him against the Christian religion: and his attachment to some Platonic sophists, who had been employed in his education, gave him as violent a bias towards Paganism. He was ambitious; and Paganism, in some of its theurgic rites, had flattered and encouraged his views of the diadem. He was vain, which made him aspire to the glory of re-establishing the ancient rites: he was extremely knowing, and fond of Grecian literature; the very soul of which, in his opinion, was the old theology: but above all, notwithstanding a considerable mixture of enthusiasm, his superstition was excessive, and what nothing but the blood of *hecatombs* could appease.

With these dispositions he came to the empire, and consequently with a determined purpose of subverting the Christian, and restoring the Pagan worship. His predecessors had left him the repeated experience of the inefficacy of downright force. The *virtue* of the *first* Christians then rendered this effort fruitless; the *numbers* of the

* A rudimentis pueritiæ primis inclinatus erat erga numinum cultum, paulatimque desiderio rei flagrabat.—Am. Marcel. L. xxii. c. 5.

present would now have made it dangerous. He found it necessary therefore to change his ground; his knowledge of human nature furnished him with arms; and his knowledge of the faith he had abandoned, enabled him to direct those arms to most advantage.

He began with re-establishing Paganism by law, and granting a full liberty of conscience to the Christians. Yet notwithstanding, his own historian* assures us, he put on this mask of moderation and equity, for no other purpose than to inflame the dissensions of the Church. And his subsequent conduct fully justifies the historian's observation.

He then fined and banished such of the more popular clergy as had abused their power, either in exciting the people to burn and destroy pagan temples, or to commit violence on an opposite sect. And it cannot be denied that their turbulent and insolent manners deserved all the severity of his justice.

He proceeded to revoke those immunities, honors and revenues, which his uncle and cousin had granted to the clergy. He disqualified the Christian laity for bearing office in the state. But his most illiberal treatment of the Christians, was his forbidding the professors who were of that religion, to teach *humanity* and the sciences, in the public schools. His more immediate design in this, was to hinder the youth from taking impressions to the disadvantage of Paganism: his remote view, to deprive Christianity of the support of human literature. Not content with this, he endeavored even to destroy what was already written in defence of Christianity. With this view he wrote to Ecdicius, the governor of Egypt, and to Porphyry the treasurer-general, to collect up and send to him the library of George, Bishop of Alexandria, who for his cruelty and tyranny had been torn in pieces by the people.

* It is not thought necessary to quote here the authorities which Warburton faithfully subjoins to his assertions.

Nay, to such a length did his aversion to the name of *Christ* carry him, as to decree by a public edict that his followers should no longer be called Christians, but *Galileans*. A man so transported by a train of the most ungoverned passions, we may well suppose, would stop at no means, how low and vile soever, to carry on his projects. His letters afford us an instance of one so dishonorable, that no testimony but his own could make it credible. Titus, Bishop of Bostra, and his clergy, in an address presented to Julian, acquaint him with their care in keeping the flock committed to them (then equal in number to the Pagans) in due obedience to the laws. The return Julian makes for this act of duty, is to acquaint the people of Bostra, that their Bishop was become their delator; that he had represented them as prone to sedition, and even capable of the last excesses, but that he and his clergy kept them in order. For this crime therefore, which he calls the taking to himself the merit of the people's good behavior, he advises them to expel the Bishop from their city.

On pretence that the Arian church of Edessa was too rich, and had not used the Valentinians with temper, he seized on every thing belonging to it, and divided the plunder amongst his soldiers. And, to add the bitterness of contumely to his injustice, he told them he did it to ease them of their burthens, that they might proceed more lightly, and with less impediment in their journey to heaven.

But Socrates, the historian, tells us, that he imposed a tax or tribute, proportioned to every man's circumstances, on all who would not sacrifice. This was persecution in form; and yet it did not stop here, but proceeded to still greater extremities. Though he did not persecute to death by laws, that being directly contrary to his edicts of toleration, which he had with so much ostentation and frequency repeated: yet he connived at the *fury* of the people, and the *brutality* of the governors of provinces, who, during his short reign, brought many martyrs to the stake. For he put such into governments whose inhumanity and blind zeal for their country superstitions were most distinguished. And when the suffering Churches presented their complaints to him, he dismissed them with cruel scoffs; telling them, their religion directed them to suffer without murmuring. So that we have little reason to doubt what the ancients say of his declared intentions (had he returned victorious from the Persian war), to subject the whole Christian world to the honester persecution of fire and sword.*

* For the account of the failure of the attempt to rebuild the Temple at Jerusalem and the apparently miraculous, certainly providential, circumstances of that failure, the reader is referred to the lengthened and ingenious argument of Bishop Warburton (*in loco citato*).

THE

EMPEROR JULIAN.

SECTION I.

CHRISTIANITY IN RELATION TO THE AGE IN WHICH IT FIRST APPEARED AND WAS PROPAGATED.

God hath made of one blood all nations of men for to dwell on all the face of the earth, and hath determined the times before appointed, and the bounds of their habitation; that they should seek the Lord, if haply they might feel after him, and find him, though he be not far from every one of us: for in him we live, and move, and have our being.—ACTS xvii. 26–28.

No new epoch is wont to commence in the history of mankind without having been previously announced by some signs or other; no truth, deeply affecting the life of men, has ever been widely spread, which individual witnesses, in their struggle with the age that was not yet ripe for it, have not expressed. So also, on the other side, it comes to pass, that individuals attempt to bring back a state of things which is no longer adapted to human society. They set themselves afresh and with great energy to give expression to that which can no longer retain its dominion over men. The old and the new are thus displayed in lively contrast and opposition to each other, and the discovery is made, how little it is in the power of an individual to *create* any thing, and how little an individual can avail in a contest with Providence, guiding and fashioning the spirit of the times according to its own everlasting decrees.

We see an example of this in the Emperor Julian. Inasmuch as he endeavored to make that *improved* form which polytheism had assumed before its final fall, the dominant religion, and opposed it to Christianity, we must speak, first of all, of the causes through which the ancient polytheistic religion again acquired new strength; of the relative position in which it stood to Christianity; of the opposition which it made thereto, and of the victory achieved against it, for which the change in the human mind had prepared the way.

The Apostle Paul says, that God left the Gentiles to themselves for a definite time to seek after God by their own strength; and, certainly (since "in him we live, and move, and have our being") men every where felt and found a divine power, as soon as they awoke from their rude and brutal condition, and arrived at the perception of an *unknown* God. But to this higher feeling and aspiration there was opposed, both externally and internally, a lower and heterogeneous nature. Endued therefore with an understanding that wished to comprehend and seek after unity and clearness, and not content with that mere feeling, man strove to justify and excuse himself for bringing the higher, godlike world (in spite of mutual opposition) into union with the heterogeneous lower world; thinking thus to get rid of the opposition.*

Now after the human understanding had finished its first career, and had exhausted itself in various attempts to deduce a *higher* and a *lower* from one common principle, and to explain the supposed process, it began to survey the structures it had raised. At once man became conscious that all these systems rested upon an *hypothesis*, and that there was no common criterion whereby to test the various systems that stood in opposition to each other,—none, at least, that was not in its turn an hypothesis, and, as such, opposed to other different hypotheses.

This was expressly announced by Skepticism, as it was exhibited before and after the appearance of Christianity; "The skeptic," says Sextus Empiricus,† "who compared together the different theories of men in order to find out a criterion

* See APPENDIX I. † *Hypotypos*, Lib. I. c. 12.

whereby to test them, and so to attain to peace of mind, perceived that by their mutual antagonism they maintained a reciprocal counterpoise; and thus, for want of the required criterion, he withheld his decision altogether." While Skepticism, in this manner, endeavored to make the human understanding itself destroy its own varied attempts to arrive at an objective certainty, it referred man back to that which subsists independently of all exposition (viz. the immediate sphere of experience and life), as the highest point to which he could with safety ascend. For its efforts were not directed against *Nature* and the *impressions*, simply and in themselves, made by her upon men, nor yet against any *appearances* of the bodily or spiritual world; but only against the *judgments* and *opinions* of the understanding respecting those appearances, as far as they affected to be any thing more than a subjective expression of individual feeling, or laid claim to a discovery of objective truth. It took good heed, in combating one species of dogmatism, not to fall into another of a negative kind, while it sought to explain away that which claimed any kind of power over men, independent of their various notions.

Its aim, on the contrary, was directed only against the expositions of men, and therefore quite as much against the negative dogmatism of unbelief in nature and religion, as against the opposite positive dogmatism in respect to both. Its object was to combat the arrogance of the dogmatic philosopher.* It did not maintain that the impossibility of arriving at objective certainty originated in the nature of things, in and by themselves; but that that uncertainty was the subjective impression made by the contemplation of human systems and conceptions on the mind of the skeptic† philosopher. It raised its views so little above what was subjective, that it did not so much as dare to determine of itself, whether it would always be in the same way of thinking, on account of the variableness of the human understanding, and its liability to veer about in all directions.‡

Sextus very happily compared this purely polemic indication of skepticism with a ladder by which a man ascends to a certain height, and after attaining a footing there kicks it down again.§ The only thing, therefore, which the skeptic did not attempt to refute was the subjective perception and consciousness of each one; though it was only by elevating this to the rank of an objective universal impression, that his un-

* Τὴν προπετεῖαν τῶν δογματικῶν. Sextus Empir.

† *Hypotypos*, Lib. I. c. 20.

‡ Διὰ τὸ πολύτροπον ἀνθρωπίνης διανοίας. L. II. *adv. Logic.* p. 546, Ed. Fabric.

§ p. 547.

derstanding could grasp the idea; "for as no one can convince him who rejoices that he does not rejoice, or him who grieves that he does not grieve, so no one can render his conviction doubtful who feels himself convinced." The skeptic applied this not only to nature, but also to that which alone concerns us at present, viz., religion. He disputed, first of all, the different expositions which philosophers gave of the origin of divine worship among men, because they all presupposed the idea of the Godhead, which nevertheless served as one and the same foundation for all the different notions of men.

"All men have one common, fundamental idea of the Deity, as a happy, imperishable Being, raised above all reach of evil; and it is perfectly unreasonable to assert that they could all by some accident have discovered these same properties, without being brought thereto by a *natural necessity*." Now skepticism certainly did not consider this idea (inherent as it is in the human mind, and inexplicable in its origin) as an irrefutable evidence of the being of a God; but its object was merely to demonstrate the impossibility of explaining the source of the idea, in reply to the different dogmatic systems; while, on the other side, it placed, over against each other, the different arguments for and against the being of a God, and showed that they reciprocally destroyed each other, by demonstrating the denial of the Deity to be attended with the same difficulties. In this instance also it was only combating the arrogance of the philosophic systems.

But where did the skeptic seek for a firm footing in actual life, that he might not (to resume my former illustration) hang floating *in the air*, after having at length mounted to the highest round of his ladder, and having thrown it away because he had no farther need of it? Truly, he clung to that which, by his own confession, was unassailable to him and preceded all those opinions and systems, viz., the immediate experience of common life. "That which causes man to act without his *willing* it and by *natural* necessity, does not admit of examination; he follows the impression and perceptions of the senses, and these, as such, are matters of certainty to him. The act of inquiry does not commence till he asks, in respect to some object, whether these perceptions actually correspond with things external to him. The skeptic, therefore, like every one else, follows those impressions, and, generally speaking, even the prevailing traditionary notions concerning divine worship, though he can as little explain their origin as he can that of the perceptions of the senses; nay, he presumes as little to pass any objective sentence or judgment upon them."*

* Lib. I. *Hypot.* Cap. 11.

"The skeptic," says Sextus, "proceeds, probably, the most securely of all philosophers, since, in accordance with the laws and regulations of his country, he allows the existence of the gods, and observes every thing that concerns their worship and the practice of piety; but he does not allow himself to be seduced into the arrogance of philosophic investigation."* "So, again," says the same representative of the skepticism of that period,† "while we follow *life* as we find it, we say that there are gods; we honor them and believe in their providential care, but we do so without any definite *meaning*."

Undoubtedly the skeptic, in thus disclaiming all express meaning, wished to secure a state of indolent repose,‡ and to comply with the impressions of actual life only so far as was necessary, without allowing himself to be disturbed by opinions relating to the good and the evil of life.§ This lukewarmness, however, could not be agreeable to the human mind, which naturally seeks for something that will warm and fill it; and this irresolute love of repose was not suited for the storms of life, especially in the frequently unhappy days of the government of the Roman emperors.

When skepticism had showed men in this way the invalidity of their received opinions, and exposed to

* p. 560. † Lib. III. Cap. 1.

‡ Ἀταραξία. § Lib. I. *Hypot.* c. 12.

them the contradiction that existed in the various philosophical systems, they saw, on the other hand, the ever-spreading fruit of theoretical and practical unbelief in the prevailing immorality of actual life; they therefore clung *in earnest*, as to the only rule of life, to the religion of their fathers, which for so many generations had propagated itself independent of human speculation, while it promoted and maintained purity of manners and the well-being of the state.*

Minucius Felix, an apologist for Christianity in the third century, introduces the heathen Cæcilius pleading for the old religion. In order to recommend that religion, he argues from the fruitless efforts of the most celebrated philosophers to discover any thing certain respecting providence and the government of the universe; and from the contradiction in which these doctrines stood to the realities of life; where we see only Nature pursuing its appointed course without any regard to men, but do not see a providence discriminating between good men and bad. "Since therefore the impotency of human nature is so far removed from the investigation of divine things, and since a fixed destiny or an inscrutable nature appears to rule over us, is it not (he asks) better and more dignified to receive the teaching of our forefathers as the criterion of truth; to observe the religious rites that have been

* See APPENDIX II.

handed down to us; to *worship* the gods whom we have been taught to *fear* before we were well able to distinguish; and, whilst we do so, to pronounce no precise judgment concerning them, but believe the account given by our fathers, who in times of ignorance and soon after the commencement of the world were even thought worthy to have the gods for their rulers or their friends?"

Listen again to a genuine description of the beneficial working of their religion, suggested by the feeling of a generation which had passed from fluctuating doubt to a firm belief, and longed again for the temples of their fathers: "The prophets, filled with the Deity with whom they are most intimately connected, foretell the future, give us warnings of approaching dangers, remedies in sickness, hope in affliction, help in distress, consolation in sudden misfortunes. In our sleep we see, hear, and acknowledge the gods whom in the light of day we wickedly deny or offend by perjury; and therefore it is, that the unanimous conviction of all nations in regard to the immortal gods remains so fixed, though men's *notions of religion* are so unsettled and the origin of religion uncertain. I have no patience, then, with any one who is so puffed up with a rash and mischievous impertinence as to strive to explain away or render doubtful so ancient, so useful, and so salutary a religion."

A tone of mind like this must have made men more sensible than ever to the claims of a new religion that could satisfy all the spiritual wants of mankind, and afford certain information as to the relation in which God stands to men. But, on the other hand, it would also excite a violent struggle for the old religion; since even infidelity and immorality, and the decay of social order, were attributed to the departure from a religious system interwoven with all the relations of society and hallowed by the duration of centuries. And to what must this lead, but a falling off into fluctuating uncertainty or a senseless dream!—for what an act of presumption must it have appeared, "that uneducated, ignorant men, deficient even in the ordinary sources of information, should presume to speak with any certainty upon subjects the most important and exalted, above which so many schools of philosophy had disputed with each other for so many ages!"* For two things are clear; first, that the Gospel was first of all made known to persons who most wanted divine instruction; and secondly, that Christianity differed from all previous religions by a decided and clear communication of religious knowledge.

Those very persons, however, who clung so fondly to the ancient religion on the ground that it had brought back again an acknowledged necessity of some

* Cæcil. in Minuc. Felix: work entitled *Octavius*.

link that should once more attach to heaven the fluctuating affections of man, these same persons (if they could but conquer their prejudices) must have been the more accessible to a religion, which offered them something more than an indistinct feeling of an intercourse with the gods, which gave them what they so much wanted, such a clear and certain conviction of the relation in which *man* stands to the Deity as can set the heart at rest, and satisfy its yearnings. In fact, as soon as Cæcilius heard those doctrines which are most intelligible to the *heart* ("and which are more easily apprehended than expressed in words"*), when he heard them clearly propounded and developed, he was convinced of the truth of Christianity, which he had hitherto considered only through the medium of preconceived opinions. Whether this conversation (in Minucius Felix) was actually held, or was only the assumed form in which the apologist clothed his arguments, at all events the occasion for it arose from the circumstances of the age, and it may so far serve for a fair characteristic thereof.

One result of that adherence to the external religion of their fathers (and this from the absence of any *living knowledge* in connection with that worship, and from the loss of all belief in any association with truth and with heaven) was a great prevalence of supersti-

* Quæ facilius est sentire quam dicere.

tion ; for superstition is merely the recovery of the lost feeling of man's relationship to God, active and energizing in the inner man. Hence the seeking for God every where in *externals* only ; hence the anxious fear of God, whom man looks upon as a Being estranged from him, always angry and vindictive ; hence the eager search after all sorts of external* methods of appeasing the Deity.

Thus, the men of that period, no longer trusting to the sole power of the decayed religion of their fathers, sought in the practices of foreign religions (which the then active and general intercourse of the far-extended Roman Empire helped to spread) all kinds of methods for propitiating the Deity ; and those methods which were the most strange gave them the greatest degree of confidence. Let us listen to Plutarch's lively picture of this sort of people in his time :† "When they meet with any kind of misfortune they do not think of looking for the cause in themselves, nor in the attendant circumstances; but always in the Deity, from whom it came down as a penal infliction. They call themselves not unfortunate, but god-hated men. Every sickness, every loss of property, every political calamity, is considered as a stroke aimed at them by a god, or as an assault of some demon. They dare not, there-

* Ἐθελοθρησκεῖα, will-worship, in its proper sense.

† Π. δεισιδαιμ. c. 3.

fore, have recourse to any assistance, lest they should appear to contend with God, or seem desirous of opposing themselves to his punishment. The physician is rejected by the sick man, and the door of the mourner is shut against the exhortation and consolations of the philosopher. 'Leave me,' (he would cry) —'me, that am accursed, me, the hated of gods and demons, to suffer the full punishment of my wickedness.' The victim of superstition is seen sitting outside his house, hung round with sordid rags, and oftentimes even rolling naked in the mire, in order to atone for his sin in having eaten or drunk some forbidden thing, or for having set his foot upon a path prohibited by the Deity."

Let us imagine the effect produced by the first Christians, when they made known the power of the Holy Ghost to men like these, encompassed by a peculiar atmosphere which their own conceits had drawn around them; when they announced to them (and proved by deeds) that the name of Christ, combined with *faith*, would deliver them from the dominion of all evil; when, by mighty works operating upon their senses, they first of all destroyed the delusion that had enveloped and rendered them inaccessible to all the arguments of reason: and setting out from thence, with simple words, preached to them the absurdity of demon-worship, reconciliation with the living God, and the power of faith to set them free. Let us listen now to the words of St. Paul (Col. ii. 20), addressed to a society of persons among whom were to be found many such converts to Christianity: "Wherefore,* if ye be dead in Christ to the elements of the world, renounce such dogmas as if ye were still entangled in the life of the world: Touch not *this;* taste not, handle not *that;* for such conduct brings destruction on him who presumes to use these things profanely—as it is expressed in the ordinances and doctrines of men. All this has, indeed, the appearance of a peculiar hidden wisdom, in an arbitrary will-worship, self-humiliation, and bodily inflictions, but relates to nothing essential, only to things merely external. Therefore, if ye be risen with Christ, seek *that which is above,* where Christ sitteth on the right hand of God. Direct your thoughts to that which is above, not to that which is earthly; for ye are dead, and your *life is hidden* with Christ in God." In this manner it was, that not this or that particular kind of superstition was refuted, but the very root thereof was at once destroyed; the heart and mind were raised from the visible world of sense to the living God; and men were powerfully reminded of the indissoluble covenant into which He had entered with them through Christ.

* It will be seen that I have here given St. Paul's language according to the German in Dr. Neander's book, not according to our own version.—*Translator.*

We have to notice yet another direction which skepticism gave to the mind of men. Its efforts were pointed (as we have already seen) against every human opinion that laid claim to objective truth; while, on the other hand, it confessed its entire impotency against that subjective conviction and feeling which lay quite out of its jurisdiction. Now this conviction, unattainable to the grasp of skepticism, was courted by distinguished men; not merely that personal, subjective feeling, before which skepticism was made to halt, but that which is to every man most *properly* and *inwardly* his own; and this, only because it is founded upon the universal moral nature of man, or on the general affinity of man's spirit to God, and lies beyond all power of thought. Skepticism soon remarked the inexplicability of one idea of the Godhead serving as a foundation for the different religious systems of such different men; but as it it did not raise its views above the personal, subjective conviction, it pursued the matter no further. It inquired not whether this idea were of that kind which would carry in itself the proof of its reality, but placed it in that class of things "which may become subjects of thought, without gaining thereby any real existence, like the Centaurs and Scylla." This inquiry, therefore, concerning the *idea* of God, would necessarily lead men to discuss His actual *existence*.* Skepticism, however, neither went deep enough, nor raised its views high enough to understand that *the idea of the Deity*, as it exists in man, is itself an incontrovertible testimony to the divine *existence;* because man *finds* nothing, in the world in which he lives, from whence this idea might have been suggested to him (as he can *find* no figure of the Centaur or Scylla, but constructs their form arbitrarily from pre-existing parts), and therefore it can only be the immediate *revelation* of that Being, of whom it is the living image in the soul of man.

"You say," says Jamblichus,† "that you *concede* the existence of the Deity; that, however, is not a correct expression; since the acknowledgment of the gods is an inherent impression, inseparably implanted in us, co-operating with the actual efforts of the soul in search of the Supreme Good, previous to any judgment, or arbitrary decision, any thought or argumentation upon the subject."

As skepticism itself led men to seek for a higher degree of certainty to which itself could not attain, so that philosophical view, which proved man's exalted origin (and the certainty of the higher order of things for which he was formed) from the ideas that are inherent in him, and which can find nothing adequate to them in the whole creation, became, under the title

* Sextus Empiric. *adv. Physic,* p. 560. † *De Myster.* c. 3.

of Platonism, the prevailing philosophy. Just as at other times (for instance, at the epoch preceding the Reformation) when fine-spun speculation detached from actual life, and human ordinances that held captive the hearts of men, had led to skepticism, superstition and infidelity, this better philosophy for a long time again spread light* and warmth around.

Skepticism had endeavored to refute the different systems of philosophy and religion by exposing their versatility† and mutual contradiction; but the Platonic philosophy pursued the opposite direction. As it had found the revelation of the Deity universal amongst men, it considered the various systems of philosophy and religion from this middle point, with the view of discovering an inner harmony amidst the opposition of forms, and of animating afresh, by means of that internal revelation, the old traditionary religions from which the living spirit had fled.

Thus Plutarch (whom we may consider as the representative of those distinguished men and of the efforts made by them) found in all religions ancient precepts of theosophists and lawgivers, that had come down to poets and philosophers, and of which no one knew the commencement or the author, though they carried with them a strong power of conviction:‡

* Φῶς φαινόμενον ἐν αὐχμήρῳ τόπῳ. † Πολυτροπία.

‡ *De Isid. et Osirid.* c. 23.

"We do not believe that there are different gods in different nations; some barbarian and some Hellenic, some Northern and others Southern; but as sun, moon, heaven, earth, and sea, are common to all, though expressed by different names, so also one Reason orders all things, and one Providence superintends all, though different modes of divine worship, and various denominations for the gods themselves may have been legally established."

These noble-minded men undertook the labor of tracing out this manifestation of the Deity in the history of nations, and they seized with fond enthusiasm any thing which offered them a confirmation or expression of the great idea with which their own minds were filled. Man (they said) born for society and mutual intercourse, and so trained up to a habit of self-dependence, is not content with comprehending the revelation of the Most High within *his own* mind, but feels a simultaneous impulse to connect it with a social, spiritual life, in which every one who is awakened to the true consciousness of his own capabilities, may be drawn up from the earthly to a higher existence. *That*, before all things, assumes with him a certain and determinate existence, which yet does not originate, or appear to originate with him; but which he finds to have a perfect being of its own, independent of him or his imaginings, and by means of which his own higher intellectual consciousness is developed. As language supplies him with impressions of certainty for his lower life, that he does not "live in a world of his own, like those who dream, but in a world which is common to all,"* so will he attain to this certainty in the intercourse of this higher world through a higher language adapted for such a community. Without these traces of a divine manifestation (not always of a mere subjective kind, but existing independently of men) the history of his species would appear nothing but a circle left to itself, and revolving always within itself.

The sad consequences had been seen of a philosophy which acknowledged no divine revelation, but explained away all religious traditions as the fictions of poetry, and sought to exclude man from all connection with heaven. Thus, for instance, Euemerus of Messene derived all religious worship from the fact, that men, superior to the rude vulgar in wisdom or strength, had, with the view of maintaining a higher estimation among them, surrounded themselves with a cloud of divinity, and were afterwards honored as gods.† The Platonists, therefore, exerted themselves in opposition to such low views, and tried to bring back their cotemporaries "to the pious belief of their fathers."‡

* Heraclit. † Sextus Empir. Lib. IX. p. 552.
‡ Plutarch, *de Pyth. Orac.* c. 13.

Let us hear with what enthusiasm Plutarch describes the pleasure of public worship which they who lived in the old faith still enjoyed: "No residence in the temples, no festivities, nothing that we ever do or see, delights us more than what we see or do in the worship of the gods, assisting at the festive dances, sacrifices, or mysteries. The soul at such times is not sad, depressed or melancholy, as it must be if it had to do with tyrannical or vindictive powers; but in those places where it thinks and believes the Deity most especially present, there it most effectually banishes all pains, and fears, and cares, giving itself up to an intoxication of pleasure, to sport and play."

With this effusion let his description of the unbeliever be compared, a description prompted by profound feeling: "All this pleasure is wanting to him who has lost all faith in a superintending Providence; for surely it is not the abundance of wine and meat that causes men's enjoyment of the festivals, but the well-grounded hope and belief that the god is propitiously present and graciously receives their offering. But if the god is not present at the sacrifice, every thing seems forsaken of heaven; the festival has miscarried with all its exalted pleasure; all is joyless and painful, since out of fear of the multitude he makes a show as if he prayed and adored the gods, without in fact praying at all, or else, in words which are contradictory to his system of philosophy; and when he brings a sacrifice, the officiating priest appears to him to be nothing but a cook or a butcher."*

But an attempt was also made to trace back the unbelief that had arisen to its cause, and it was attributed to the extinction of the true spirit of religion; to the coarse, anthropomorphistic representations of the operations of the gods; or to the materialistic process of amalgamating the organs and symbols of the gods and their operations, with the gods themselves and their immediate works; a confusion and mixture which must necessarily have shocked man's understanding, and rendered the whole of religion a matter of suspicion, as something contradictory and the invention of ignorant, uninformed men. "When men," says Plutarch, "accustomed themselves to speak of brazen or stone images, and of pictures, not *as images* and *instruments* for honoring the gods, but as *actual gods,* they gradually received into their minds the perverted representations involved in such expressions; and it was exactly this confusion of words and things which plunged men of weak and amiable minds into boundless superstition, but strong and daring dispositions, on the contrary, into atheistic, wild opinions."

The attempt was now made, by taking an intellectual view of the subject, to make the conflicting spirits

* Non posse suaviter vivi sec. Epicur. c. 22.

of unbelief and superstition work well together; and this view, which sought to vindicate the old religion against all objections by bringing it into harmony with the ideas of reason and the laws of the understanding, produced a new form of *religious* philosophy.

After Plutarch had shown* that the same eternal religion, only under different forms, was to be found in all nations, he thus proceeds: "Some make use of darker, others of clearer, sacred symbols, which lead the mind to the Divine Being, though not without danger; for some, missing that intended use altogether, fell away into superstition, while others, shunning that as a dangerous slough, plunged at last into the abyss of unbelief. Therefore we must borrow for our assistance the precepts of philosophy that lead to holiness, that we may not misunderstand the wise appointments of the laws concerning sacrifice." The object aimed at thereby was, "that, on one hand, the excellent old regulations should not be abandoned, and, on the other, that the traditionary notions of the gods should not be disturbed and perplexed by strange and inappropriate representations."

As superstition mixes and confounds the divine and the human causes, natural and supernatural, the instrument and the efficient principle, the objective and the subjective, one with another; whilst unbelief, on the

* *De Iside et Osiride*, c. 67.

contrary, recognizes only the human, the natural and the subjective;—(both parties erring in this, that they do not properly separate and discriminate this twofold combination)—so those good men endeavor to avoid both these devious paths, by marking accurately the relation of the divine and heavenly to the human and the natural, of the subjective to the objective, of the spirit to the letter. "The oldest theosophists and poets," says Plutarch,* "saw every where only the Deity itself in active operation, and paid no regard to the indispensable natural causes; the succeeding philosophers, on the contrary, who first discovered those natural causes, wished to explain every thing thereby, and nowhere acknowledged a divine operative principle."

Inquiries were now entered upon which had hitherto been unknown to polytheism (a religion so averse to all that is dogmatic), viz., concerning revelation, inspiration, and miracles. Accordingly, at this, as at all times when these subjects have become matters of discussion, two opposite parties arose. One party made use of the meanness of the Pythia's verses as a proof that the whole affair was of human contrivance, and certainly the work of no god; the other maintained that even the *language* in which the god disclosed the future, was necessarily the most beautiful because it originated from God; and that nothing but the cor-

* *De defectu Orac.* c. 48.

rupted taste of men hindered them from acknowledging this beauty as superior to every thing human, in its simplicity and sublimity. A third party of these religious philosophers, differing from both, sought to settle this dispute by analyzing the notion of revelation and inspiration, by distinguishing the matter from its mode of expression, the mere instrument from the higher power that makes use of it.

"From the Deity proceeds only the matter, the higher influence, the inspiration; he communicates the ideas to the soul and excites the light within it, but neither the language, nor the expression, nor the metre, comes from him.* The distinct individuality of the human agents need not be annihilated by this divine influence; but every being, whom the Deity makes use of as its instrument, can communicate the divine will conformably to his individual endowments, and any defect in the mode must not therefore be ascribed to the God who employs it."† A difference therefore in these revelations was deduced from the difference in the instruments through which they were conveyed to men, sometimes pure and free from alloy, sometimes more combined with human frailty, and obstructed by the natural causes through which they operate. "The soul" (says Plutarch, *loc. cit.*) "is the organ or instru-

* *De Pyth. Orac.* c. 5 et seqq. † c. 21.

ment of the Deity, and the efficacy of an instrument consists in representing (as far as is possible, according to its peculiar ability) the higher power that operates by its means, and in revealing the thoughts of that power; not indeed in perfect purity and free from all *passions* and all *defects*, as those thoughts are, but mixed with much that is extraneous. For every thing pertaining to the Deity *in and by itself* is beyond our power of vision, and when it reveals itself to us through some other agent, it mixes itself up with the proper nature of that agent."

He thence beautifully explains how the violent ecstasy of inspiration resulted from the contest of two opposite emotions, the higher divine one communicated to the individual, and the natural one proper to the individual himself; just as an uneasy struggle between the natural and the communicated motion is produced in bodies to which, while by their nature they gravitate to the earth, a circular movement has been communicated.

It is worth while to remark the manner in which Plutarch justifies the alteration in the language of the oracles as adapted, according to the plan of Providence, to the altered language and the civilization of nations. "In the earliest times," he says,* "men might have loved what was splendid and striking in their

* Plut. *de Pyth. Orac.* c. 25.

dress, their language, and in all the concerns of life; poetry may have been the language of common life, while the use of type and enigma may have given to things a divine and holy aspect in the eyes of that race of men; but now, on the contrary, men have come to like nothing but what is simple and intelligible, whilst any lofty flights of poetry or of mystery would excite a suspicion of an attempt to deceive." He has here, though unconscious of it himself, confessed that the alteration in the culture of the human mind would produce a desire for religious instruction adapted to that advancement.

It was the aim of those of whom we are at present speaking, to recall men's notions of religion from the general abstractions of the philosophers and sophists into the concerns of actual life, and to give to religion renewed warmth and efficiency. From a dislike to what was merely human, some philosophers had spun out and refined their ideas of religion still farther into generalities, and thereby deprived it of all that was practical and influential. In thus acting, they did not remember that when man forms his abstractions from himself as God's image, he at once cuts off all support from beneath his feet, and falls, if not into a materializing, certainly a formal and empty anthropomorphism. Many a one fancied that the idea of a Providence extending to every individual concern, however transitory, savored too much of human machinery; that the free agency of every individual could not consist with the eternal, unalterable law by which the world is governed; and that the Deity cares only for the preservation of the universe and its various species of existences, while the routine of the world is repeated, according to an eternal law, with an unchangeable necessity.* Some again imagined that the Supreme Spirit lived only in the eternal act of self-contemplation; because, if he contemplated any thing external to himself, he must necessarily† go out of himself.‡ It was in opposition then to this refinement and generalization of religion, that these men of warmer feelings endeavored to turn men's religious notions into a living, active, invidualizing principle.

From these well-meant efforts there also naturally resulted an enthusiastic fondness for a Polytheism combined with the philosophic idea of the Divine Unity. The idea of a Divine Being, as it appeared to the men of those days, resembled one of those cold and refined abstractions of philosophy, by means of which they wished to simplify and, in point of fact, to metamorphose every thing. Much warmer therefore to the mind, and much more animating to the imagination, was the notion, that the One Supreme Deity§ not only

* Just. Mart. *Dial. c. Tryph. Jud.* init.

† Plut. *de defectu Orac.* c. 30. et Aristot. *Metaph.*

‡ See APPENDIX III.

§ Zeus, or Jupiter.

lived in the enjoyment of a happy existence, but had produced from himself other beings of a like nature, with whom he shared his happiness, and through whom he extended his operative power in a descending scale down to man himself. As therefore they considered Him as the supreme,* essential good, so they thought these created deities were partial manifestations of that good. The living idea of every virtue and every faculty was personified in some one deity; nor could it be conceived that the fairest virtue of equitable and friendly intercommunion, which assigns to each one that which is his own, could be wanting to the Supreme Being; the *beau ideal* of a society and of a spiritual community being identified with the assembly of the gods. "There are," says Plutarch,† "besides the One Supreme, several other deities, towards whom he exercises the virtues proper to a community."

This effort directed against philosophical abstractions and simplifications, is plainly manifested in the manner in which the existence of a plurality of worlds is proved; for instance in Plutarch,‡ who asserts, "that one *isolated* world does not revolve, in a void waste, round endless space; that God does not look upon a boundless *vacancy* external to himself, nor does he contemplate himself only and nothing else; but he

* *αὐτὸ τὸ ἀγαθόν.* † *De Defect. Orac.* c. 4. ‡ *loc. cit.* c. 20.

views the actions of many gods and men, and the motions and revolutions of many planets in their appointed periods: since the Deity does not dislike such variation, but rather rejoices therein."

In the same manner objection was made to those systems which exhibited an *endless* number of worlds; because the mind turns giddy before the boundless view, which appears to it as if it were connected with a blind chance; just as the uniform sameness of the opposite view appeared to it a dead and empty void. In the gods, "who were not inclosed in matter nor subject with it to alteration, but free and exalted above it, guided and directed it as the helmsman steers the vessel,"*—in the gods was exhibited the perfection of free-agency, which in mortals is only found under limitation. With a view of reconciling philosophical ideas with the Greek theosophy, a distinction was made between the invisible gods themselves and the visible, permanent forms in which they revealed themselves; and to the confused notion of these two ideas, entertained by the common people, was attributed the wide diffusion of perverted representations of the nature of the gods.

Thus, in the regular course of the stars and their influence upon the earth, a proof was supposed to be discovered of the operation of a divine reason, not

* c. 29.

confined (like that of man) by any connection with matter, but controlling it in perfect freedom. For instance, the image of the active energy of the god Apollo in the celestial world was seen in the powerful influence of the visible sun (Helios) in the world of sense; and just as the sun's light adapts itself to the eye in which the power of vision has been brought to great perfection, so Apollo can exhibit himself to the mental eye of him, whose higher faculties he has excited to superior activity.* "The sun however withdrew men in general from thus recognizing Apollo, since through the medium of the senses it turned away the human mind from the true sight of him in his revealed symbol to that symbol itself in its visible appearance."†

We cannot, says Plutarch, but regard and love those who attach the idea of the Deity to an object which they esteem as the most dear and valuable of all they are acquainted with. Since however they obtain a representation of the Deity only in a dream (though the most beautiful of all dreams), they are obliged to elevate that representation to something far above it and every thing visible; and thus they are enabled to contemplate the Deity imaged in his visible representation, and admire the life-giving power which (as far as the visible can express the spiritual) presents to them

* *De Defect. Orac.* c. 12. † *De Pyth. Orac.* c. 12.

a faint picture of the life and happiness of the god himself.*

Now these men of higher intellectual cultivation certainly introduced purer religious ideas into the popular worship; they honored in the different deities only one Divine Being, who revealed himself through them. They looked upon their images as nothing but images, and endeavored to remove every thing of a material nature from the pure idea of the Godhead; and as for auspices and auguries, they considered them only as the operations of an omnipresent Providence, which gave men tokens concerning the future through the medium of natural causes that were subject to its will.† "A knowledge of the laws of nature (Plutarch thus remarks) needs not be opposed at all to a belief in auspices and auguries. The natural philosopher may

* De EI, apud *Delph.* 21. This word EI was a somewhat mysterious inscription in the temple at Delphos, and forms the title and subject of one of Plutarch's treatises, written in the form of a conversation. It was one of three inscriptions on conspicuous parts of the temple, and intended probably, like the other two (Γνῶθι σεαυτὸν and Μηδὲν ἄγαν), to convey warning or instruction. This word EI was repeated by subsequent worshippers in various materials: *e. g.* by Livia Augusta in gold, and by the Athenians in brass. The discussion in Plutarch gives the various explanations of the party, some trifling enough. The most reasonable are, first, that as the god seemed to exhort the worshippers with Γνῶθι σεαυτὸν, the worshipper was thus admonished to reply Εἰ, "Thou art;" or, as some expressed it, Εἰ ἕν, "Unum es: non multa." Secondly, that it suggested *prayer:* Εἰ for εἴθε, "O that!"—*Translator.*

† Compare Plut. *Pericl.* c. 6.

know the natural origin and the actual circumstances, while the augur understands the special object and purpose of the phenomena, as tokens, or signs of something else. Those persons who supposed that together with a knowledge of the cause the phenomenon must cease to be a sign, did not observe that, according to this mode of judging, all the representations of actual objects by human art would also cease to be *signs* as soon as the cause of their production was known."

The religious knowledge of the multitude however was not thereby enlightened. They could not raise their thoughts to those intellectual views; while that which struck their eyes retained its hold upon them, from the impression which the accompanying circumstances made on them through the senses. Whilst, therefore, that enlightened view produced (with the few) a new enthusiasm for the old religion, and even led to the adoption of symbols from foreign religions, the grossest superstition was promoted among the common people. It was proved on this, as on many other occasions, that no religious reformation can ever be effected by little and little through the progressive influence of intellectual cultivation, though it may thereby be accelerated and prepared for. Even when so much inflammable matter has accumulated in the intellectual atmosphere, the spark must still be thrown into it that is to set it in a blaze.

The case was similar at the time of the Reformation, but with this difference; that then for the first time appeared the only medium through which Christianity could be resuscitated, viz., a general extension of religious knowledge at once active and clear. Ingenious men can generally combine that pre-existing matter with their own view of the subject, and adapt their measures to it; and this occurred as well at the period of which we are speaking as in the history of Romanism. For instance, all the three contending parties in the dispute about image-worship had, in point of fact, correct notions about the living God and his worship, though the question produced one of those discrepancies that are grounded on the imperfection of human nature. One party sought to raise itself *mentally* to the Invisible, and disdained the use of an image, as something as far below the dignity of the Invisible, as it tended to draw down the mind to mere sense, and gave occasion to superstitious practices.* Another party would have the image to serve only as a remembrancer of the Invisible. The third party, with whom feeling predominated over reason and un-

* Even as early as the beginning of the age we are treating of there arose an opposer of image-worship, in the person of a learned Roman, Varro, who deduced the corruption of religion among the Romans from the introduction of iconolatry. He asserted that those who first set up images of the gods had removed all piety from the state, and caused the spread of new errors.—Aug. *de. Civ. Dei,* Lib. iv. c. 13, Note 6.

derstanding, looked upon the image as glorified by the Invisible whom they felt to be there present; and therefore in that image they worshipped the unseen Deity that resided in it. But there was then (as there always is) this disadvantage attending the use of symbols and types, that the common people forgot the invisible original in his image, and lost sight of him altogether in the contemplation of his external symbol; whilst very few paid any attention to the image of God in the heart of man, and the revelation he makes of himself, in the business of life.

But now, in how strong a contrast to this religion (connected as it was with so many dazzling symbols and images addressed to the mind as well as the senses) must Christianity have appeared, revealing only the Invisible One in his original purity, and rejecting every other image, every other temple than that which exists in the heart of man! "Though half naked themselves," says Cæcilius of the Christians, (in Minucius Felix,) "they despise the pomp and purple of the priests. Why have they no altars, no temples, no recognized images?"

Those more intellectual men, above mentioned, certainly declared that all external rites, all images and symbols, were unprofitable without a knowledge of the truth; but still they considered them to be necessary in order to lead men to the truth, and as means of purification, through which men became susceptible of the influence of the gods. It was indeed acknowledged that "it was not external, symbolical rites, nor the shorn head and linen dress, that made the priest of Isis." It was asserted that the inquiry after the truth was something more holy than all the acts of abstinence and temple-worship; yet all traditionary practices were looked upon as holy, and of undeniable authority, and so much the more so at a time when such zealous efforts were made to call back religion again to the concerns of life, and to defend its influence over individuals against the generalizations of the philosophers—that which was old and established against the attacks of infidelity. The priest was considered as alone and exclusively dedicated to the service of the gods; he was distinguished from all other men by outward dress, by solemn, symbolical acts, by withdrawing himself into the temple, by the performance* of certain rites there, and by abstinence from certain kinds of food; and all this was connected, by means of symbolic expositions, with his destination as one exclusively devoted to the knowledge and service of the Godhead.†

At a time when these notions were spreading, and would naturally mix themselves even with Christianity in its early development; when men were seeking,

* Λατρεῖαι. † Compare especially Plut. *de Iside et Osiride*.

with ardent longing, for the lost connection with Heaven, and for new revelations of its will; when practices which were adopted by individuals with a purely intellectual view, became superstitious observances with the vulgar;—St. Paul wrote to the Colossians,* exhorting them to beware lest any man should seduce them by merely human philosophy not founded upon Christ, in whom alone they had all the fulness of the Godhead revealed; and reminding them, that as Christ had conquered for them all evil and all opposing powers, they were now exalted, through him, above that which was visible, and were made free to live to him in faith only. "Let no man, therefore, judge you as to any kind of meat or drink, or in respect of a holy-day."—"Let no man triumph over your liberty by enforcing external acts of humility, and worshipping of higher spirits; prying into things which he hath never seen, in the empty pride of a mind set only upon the externals of religion."

At a subsequent date, near the end of the second century, when Christianity had now spread among a larger humber and a greater variety of men, (and had therefore been also mixed up with various human imaginations,) Tertullian asserted that, properly speaking, all Christians are priests, and all, by virtue of that

* Coloss. ii. 8–18. Here, as elsewhere, I give St. Paul's words according to Dr. Neander's version or paraphrase —*Translator.*

priesthood, had a right to administer baptism; because what all had received in the same way might also be imparted in the same manner by them to others.* And the consciousness of possessing this priestly dignity was so general and so strong among Christians, that the laity sometimes enforced it in opposition to the views and claims of the clergy, who had begun to look upon themselves as a peculiarly distinct order, devoted to God's service. Therefore Tertullian remarks†—"When we would exalt ourselves, and bear ourselves haughtily towards the clergy, then we say, *We are all one and alike*,‡ being all of us priests; for Christ hath made us all priests before God and his Father."

When the Montanists of that day wished to establish regular fasts and ascetic practices among Christians, this spirit of Christian freedom rose up in opposition. The Christians found fault with this as "a mixture of heathen superstition with Christianity; whereas the free Christian faith was not at all bound to the rules of abstinence prescribed in the Mosaic law; nor, according to the teaching of the Bible, could a man be defiled by any thing external to himself; moreover the Lord had prescribed no such fasting, no

* See Tertullian *de Baptismo.*

† *De Monogam.* c. 12, p. 581, Edit. Bas.

‡ In the Latin (as well as the German, Sind wir alle *eins*) it is more strong, *Unum* omnes sumus. See Bishop Kaye on *Eccles. Hist. of the second and third Centuries.—Translator.*

abstinence from meats, but rather abstinence from evil and from the works of legal righteousness.*

The external observances of the Christian religion, from their being both few and simple, were contrasted by the dazzling worship of the heathens; wherefore Tertullian (after speaking of the simple rite of baptism, as offering nothing striking or glittering to the senses, and liable to be despised on that very account) remarked that, on the contrary, the festivities and mysteries of heathenism procured for it both belief and respect by its processions, its preparatory rites, and its large expenditure.† Christianity at that time must have made some such an appearance in relation to the public heathen-worship, as certain sects that affected to revive the pure spirituality of Christianity, presented in comparison with the dominant Church of the middle ages.

As at that time every one, who denied the being, the agency, and the revelations of the gods (as they were traditionally taught in the popular religion) was generally called an atheist,‡ so Christianity itself became an object of hatred under the name of atheism. A religion directed purely to the Invisible, without any

* *De Jejun. advers. Psychic.* p. 771.

† *De Baptism,* c. 1.

‡ "One God is as good as none." "Unus Deus nullus est," says the Emperor Hadrian in Flavius Vopiscus Saturnin, c. ii. N. 4.

pomp of worship to attract the eye, blended with no national custom, connected with no peculiar class of citizens; a religion which bore upon it no character or mark of exclusive nationality, but claimed to produce a perfectly new creation in all who received it, and to be the religion of the human race;—such a fact as this was something that had never been thought or heard of. Judaism, therefore, was more esteemed because it was the religion of a distinct people, and quite peculiar to them, being interwoven with their political constitution, and combined with an external ceremonial worship. "Even the Jews," says Cæcilius, "a wretched people as they are, and separate from all other nations, certainly worship but one God; yet they do it openly, they do it in temples, they do it with altars, sacrifices, and ceremonies." Celsus, the opponent of Christianity, speaks thus:* "The Jews, as a distinct self-subsisting people, had a national code of laws which they also faithfully observed; their religion, such as it was, was the religion of their country; and in that respect they acted like all other men, who have continued to follow the institutions of their country, of whatever kind they may be. And this appears a useful practice, not only because the individual is bound to comply with the laws prescribed by the nation; but also, inasmuch as it is probable that at the

* Origen *c. Celsum*, Book v.

beginning of the world the different portions of the earth were allotted to different heavenly superintendents, under whose separate government those nations were respectively placed, it would clearly be a crime to do away with regulations which originally proceeded from them.*

The idea of the infinite perfectibility of nations and of individuals is quite peculiar to monotheism, which recognizes in men the image of the all-comprising Deity; so that it prescribes also one mental training for men, one system of religion and morality, to which all may be brought by education. The Polytheist imagines the ideal perfection of individual virtues and faculties to be personified in individual gods; and therefore he sees in every human being and in every nation the image of some god, of whom it is a manifestation, and to whose guidance they are subject. He sees also a decided moral and intellectual character imparted to each nation from which it cannot depart, and therefore esteems the different forms of national religion as revelations from that national god, completely blended with the distinguishing character and peculiar social institutions of the particular nation. Men hated therefore in the Jews only "the presumptuous spirit and barbarian self-conceit," with which they excluded all other gods, and declared their own

* See Appendix IV.

religion the only one, their God as the only God; while this "mixture of pride and rudeness" was thought to express itself in all their demeanor. The Romans, on the contrary, destined as they were by Heaven to rule over all other nations, for that very reason honored the gods of all nations, and received them all in a friendly spirit. "We see," says Cæcilius, "that whilst all nations and kingdoms have their national worship and honor their respective gods, the Romans respect the gods of all the others, just as their power and authority have reached the compass of the whole world. They search out every where these foreign gods, and adopt them for their own; nay, they have even erected altars to the *unknown* gods and to the infernal deities."

Christianity therefore, the extension of which had been promoted by the ruin of established institutions, was generally thought to have a tendency to cause the decay of states because it attached itself to none in particular; not to mention, that from the close connection of religion with conventional forms, a contest with the one must have involved it in a contest with the other. Christianity at once placed itself in a different position, in regard to human life, from the preexisting religions, which were so interwoven therewith and so closely related to all its circumstances. Christianity, on the contrary, looked upon this mortal life not as the object, but only as the means; bestowed upon all a relation to another and an unseen world, and taught an exalted, perfect morality, far above all human laws, to which men were then first called upon to conform their lives: this perfect moral code, and the direction which it gave to men's minds towards interests out of and above this lower world, appeared to suppress all zeal for temporal concerns, all care for the present life, and all love for their father-land. Christians therefore were spoken of as a class of persons quite unfit for the intercourse of social life;* as men who shunned the light, concealing themselves in their dark corners, dumb as soon as they are seen in public, talkative in their private haunts;† who express with unbounded freedom their disapprobation of the present state of things.‡ The Romans delighted to speak of Rome as the Everlasting City, but the Christians announced to them the coming destruction of the whole world, which was only delayed by the existence of the Roman empire, the last of all successive empires.

To these causes of disagreement were added still

* Homines infructuosos in negotiis. Tertull. *Apolog.* p. 883. Edit. Bas.

† Latebrosa et lucifugax natio, in publicum muta, in angulus garrula. Cæcilius *apud Minuc. Fel.*

‡ Quibus præsentia semper tempora cum enormi libertate displicent. Flavii Vopisc. *vita Saturnin.* c. 1,

more points in the character and genius of Christianity, in which it differed, both theoretically and practically, from the mode of thought till then universally received. Those who at that time (*e. g.* the Platonists) made an esoteric and exoteric revelation the basis of their philosophy, conceived the notion (among external sources of revelation) of a stirring up of the Divine Spirit in the inward man, varying according to the different necessities of individuals. Plutarch* therefore calls the collected mass of the various traditions and revelations,† the materials of that philosophy which had for its object the teaching of divine things.‡ According to their ideas, so-called mysteries were only such to the unitiated; but whosoever had his understanding opened to the divine influence within him, could arrive at an adequate knowledge of these symbols and revelations by following the impressions made by them on his mind. But the idea of a revelation, *confined within itself*, perfectly *new* and far surpassing man's ordinary means of information (of which man might perhaps conceive the necessity, but which, from the defect adhering to his actual acquaintance with the subject, he could not adequately comprehend,) the very idea of a revelation so decided in its character was foreign from the existing philoso-

* *De defect. Orac.* c. 2. † Ἱστορίαν. ‡ Θεολογίαν.

phy.* It gave, however, a new direction to the philosophic mind, and produced what we may call "the critique, or inquiry into the powers of the human understanding in relation to a higher kind of knowledge."

With the ancients philosophy had not generally proceeded from religion (as among Christians it proceeded from the inquiry into the capacities of man's understanding in regard to revelation), but rather from the observation of nature. Men conceived therefore of *Infinity*† that it was a predicate of matter, or rather its remaining essence, after the abstraction of all definite organization and bodily shape; in short, as something entirely defective and without form, which could not be comprehended by the human intellect, but could be arrived at only by a λόγος νόθος.‡ Therefore it was that to this *Infinity* (thus arrived at by the abstraction of all definite forms) men always attached the idea of a chaos and a blind necessity, and carefully removed the notion from God§ and divine things. This unorganized and shapeless essence, which was discovered by analyzing the notion of the corporeal world,‖ could by no process be combined with the idea

* See APPENDIX V.

† Ἄπειρον.

‡ Illegitimate reasoning, λογος for λογισμος.—*Translator.*

§ Compare Plut. *de Defec. Orac.* c. 24—30.

‖ On the one side was the ἄπειρον, on the other the πέρατα within which definite bodies exist.

of the Deity; it was therefore imagined to be that which served as a basis for the creation, and itself to have been first reduced to an organized, corporeal state by means of that same creation.*

As the notion of a Being incomprehensible to man was foreign from the then existing mode of thought, so also was the idea of an incipient creation, and the commencement of time. To this we must add another and more practical difference in the estimate of things. The natural man seeks and recognizes the Divine in the great and the extraordinary. In the regular motions of the planets, in the course of the universe, (on the whole ever uniform and consistent), he sees the manifestation of a Mind, free as to any restraint of matter, yet directing itself according to unchangeable laws; while, on the contrary, the nature of man every where exhibits to him the traces of dependence and decay. He recognizes the universe as the image of God, and man, next in order, as an image and portion of the universe.

Through the announcement of an Incarnate God the aspect of things was completely changed. The close connection between God and man was here exhibited by representing the latter as the image chosen for the manifestation of the former: he thus appeared as the centre of creation, to which every thing else

* See Appendix VI.

was related. Cæcilius therefore, in Minucius Felix, speaks thus against the Christians: "They threaten destruction to the entire world and all the stars, as if the divine order of Nature, which is founded upon eternal laws, could be disturbed. And, not content with this strange fancy, they compose old wives' fables; they assert that they return again to life after their bodies have returned to the dust. O! the twofold insanity—to announce the destruction of the heavens and the stars, which we leave behind us just as we found them! and to promise immortality to us who die as we were born! No wonder then they so abominate the *burning of the dead*." In the same manner also Celsus* derides the Christian doctrine, that all things were created for the sake of men: "All things (he says†) were created in order that the world might exist, as God's work, complete in all respects; the whole is the object of God's care; his providence never leaves it, nor does it ever become worse. God will never recall it to himself, and he is no more angry with it on account of men, than on account of the brutes."

The announced advent of the Son of God, and the whole character of his life upon earth, gave every where a new direction to the moral and religious mind of men, as well as their moral and æsthetic estimate of things; since the idea of the Divine nature "in the

* Lib. IV. Orig. c. 77. † Ibid. c. 99.

form of a servant" would never originate from the natural man.* The feeling of constraint, accompanied by the consciousness of a higher power that lies confined within him, drives him to *idealize* for himself. He seeks for and invents gods, who reveal themselves in perfect form, surrounded with light and splendor, and free from the defects and constraint under which frail human nature labors. His heroes display immense, superhuman strength, which triumphs alike over savage nature and the violence of godless men.

The idea of divine dignity combined with humility and human weakness, of power displayed in suffering, is one which man's invention never produced. St. Paul therefore had good reason for remarking (what indeed is found to be true at all times), that "Christ crucified was to the heathen foolishness;" and therefore it was that "the worshippers of a dead and crucified Master" were so despised by the heathen. The change, however, produced thereby in the moral views of society extended to all the concerns of life. Meekness coupled with strength, power united with endurance, now became the highest form of virtue; they were alike honored in the martyrs. Their sufferings and death (amidst torments that were shocking to the senses) were celebrated as a victory. All possible information respecting them was carefully collected,

* See APPENDIX VII.

as well as the remains of those bodies through which they had displayed such superhuman energy. Meetings were held on the anniversary of their suffering, which was spoken of over their tombs as their *proper birth-day*;* nay, they were still considered as partakers in the Communion of the Lord's Supper, in proof that, *in the Lord*, Christians were still united with those who died for him. Hence, too, originated the care which Christians immediately bestowed upon their sepulchres; so that Tertullian, as early as the end of the second century, remarks, that the Christians expended more money in Arabian frankincense than the heathens did in the religious service of their gods.†

But let us now also view the other side of the picture, and see how much this contrast of Christianity with the prevailing modes of moral and philosophical thought contributed to the wider spread of Christ's religion. A notion had been generally adopted among the educated classes, that *all religions* were revelations of a divine mediatorial Mind, presented under various human forms, and causing more or less trouble to the Deity.‡ This Eclecticism gave man no certainty, as he was obliged first of all to find out the Deity from amidst this admixture with its human representatives. Men therefore, being prepared by this idea for the reception of a religion which could serve as a common

* Dies natalitios martyrum. † *Apolog*. p. 884.

‡ See APPENDIX VIII.

centre to all other religions, found this now in Christianity. They recognized here the truth and the Divine Mind in the purity and completeness of its revelations. From this elevation they looked back upon all other forms of philosophy and religion, and were pleased at finding therein traces and manifestations (however isolated and detached) of that affinity of the Godhead to man which they had now found revealed in its purity and perfection. "Every one," says Justin Martyr, in the second century, who had himself gone over from the Platonic philosophy to Christianity,—"every one who recognizes in particular revelations of the Divine Word (of which the seed exists in all men) the truth which is allied thereto, teacheth correctly; but inasmuch as the philosophers have contradicted each other on the weightiest subjects, they have proved thereby that they are not in possession of sound, irrefutable knowledge; a blessing which belongs to all of us who are Christians; and all are Christians who have lived and are now living agreeably to the Divine Word."

The Platonic philosophy made men acquainted with the sublimity of the Divine nature, and its affinity to the mind of man; it excited in them a feeling of the Godlike, an elevating enthusiasm and an ardent longing to explore beyond the limits of actual life; hence arose the inclination to the magic art. To restless man, thus longing after and seeking for the truth, and painfully sensible of the defective, limited powers of human nature, Christianity pointed out a way to God by the practice of humility; and whilst it announced to him the revelation of God in the nature of man, it inspired him by that belief with a confidence that, being united with God, he might, even in that restricted state, exhibit the features of a divine race. It showed to him the perfection of virtue expressed amidst the restrictions of humanity; and thereby taught him to strive after his high destination, not in the infinity which lay beyond, but within the compass of those very restrictions. St. Augustine felt all this, when burning with thirst for truth and virtue, he passed, after long vacillation, from the new Platonic philosophy to the Christian faith: "That the Eternal Son of God* (he says) remains unchangeably exalted, before and beyond all time; that the souls of men receive all their happiness from his fulness; and that they are renewed in wisdom by their union with the wisdom that abideth eternally in him:—all this I learnt in that philosophy; but that this Son of God had come down to the human race as his own possession, and that he had given, to all who receive and believe in him, power to become the sons of God:—*this* I found not there; for Thou hast hidden these things from the wise and prudent, and revealed them unto babes, in order that those who labor and are heavy-laden may

* *Confess.* Lib. vii. c. 8—21.

come unto him, and He may give them strength." He says in another place, "It is *one thing* to look down from a wooded height upon the abode of peace, while, unable to find the way that leads to it, you strive in vain to pass through pathless tracts; it is *another thing* to have the way that leads thither made passable and safe through the victory of our heavenly Leader."

At a time of general complication, confusion, and approaching dissolution of human institutions, men had the greatest need of, and were most alive to, the impressions of a religion, which raised them above all mere visible forms; confining itself to no national and political forms, like all other religions; but uniting all men of all nations in one common faith, it formed a character till then quite new, advancing claims to universal acceptance, independent of any peculiar nationality. They were no longer the times of a free and happy social life; liberty and patriotism could no longer produce heroic virtues; it was now seen how far the influence of these human motives extended. Whoever then sought for the ideal perfection of the olden time (when men displayed themselves in the fulness of natural strength abandoned to its own discretion) must have been filled with hatred for his fellow-men from the contrast presented by actual life, or else have sunk under the sense of degradation. Every thing seemed to slacken the efforts of the human mind, and tended to reduce it to a servile state. Self-indulgence,* empty, pampered and æsthetic, was opposed to any real change of heart; all ideas of what is good and noble were reduced to a question of taste; men of rank made honor consist in the possession of busts that most resembled the sages of antiquity: they had the lofty sentiments of the ancients on their lips, and extolled with high-sounding words the virtues of ancient heroes. This outside and assumed show contented that effeminate generation; satisfied with glossing over and concealing from others (perhaps, for the time, even from themselves) their real weakness, they yet felt some degree of shame in society, possibly even by themselves. They exerted not, however, the least energy of will to bring their lives in the smallest degree into harmony with this external appearance.†

It was at this period of man's history that a religion appeared which held out to admiration no glittering *ideal* to dazzle the imagination or allure the senses of men, but showed them a pattern of virtue well calculated to impel their hearts to copy it, and to which they were both required and enabled to conform their lives. And what a religion! Whilst it, at first, called every man to a knowledge of himself, and a consciousness of his total corruption, it at the same time raised in him also a consciousness of dignity; it required no display of supposed divine relations in order

* See Persius, *Sat.* I.

† See Juvenal, *Sat.* II.

to reveal itself to him; it could present itself to him equally in all the circumstances of life, however limited. It gave man an elevated feeling that could be crushed by no human despotism, because it was grounded upon something which can neither be constrained or advanced by man; in short, it offered an appropriate remedy for all the moral diseases of the age, a consolation adapted to all its calamities. The divine power of this religion was shown in the daily life of individuals, and through their example it drew others to accept it. "We can show you," says Justin Martyr, in the second century, "many amongst us, who from having been violent and tyrannical, have become quite different characters: men, who were conquered by the force of example, while they beheld the all-enduring patience of their neighbors, or the extraordinary forbearance of their travelling companions in submitting to injury, or in any other way became acquainted with Christians in the ordinary intercourse of life." This religion inspired men with a new and different sort of heroism, a spirit which showed itself in suffering as well as in action; which, as it was not kindled by the existing circumstances of life, by the love of liberty or fame, so neither could it be suppressed or extinguished by bonds and slavery; nay, it exhibited to an enervated age tranquillity of soul amidst the acutest tortures.

SECTION II.

JULIAN'S EDUCATION, AND THE FORMATION OF HIS CHARACTER, TILL HIS ELEVATION TO THE IMPERIAL THRONE.

JULIAN, son of Constantius, a brother of the emperor Constantine, and of Basilina, daughter of an Imperial Lieutenant, already in his sixth year, saw the blood of the individuals who were nearest and dearest to him shed by violence. After the death of the emperor Constantine in the year of our Lord 337, almost all the members of the imperial family, victims of suspicion and distrust, were murdered by the soldiers, in a tumultuous excitement (as it was said), but through the secret order of the emperor Constantius, who believed that he could by that means only secure the possession of his throne. Amongst these victims Julian lost his father and his eldest brother; his second brother, Gallus, was only saved from instant death by a dangerous illness, and himself by his tender years. Abandoned by those who might have paid him more strict attention* (since his mother had been taken from him a few days after his birth), his education was intrusted to an aged tutor, Mardonius, an hereditary slave of his mother's family, whom his grandfather had

* See Julian's *Misopogon*, p. 351, 53. *Orat. ad Salust.* p. 241. *Socrat.* 3. 1. Libanius *in Jul. necem.*

brought up and educated, in order to instruct his mother in elegant literature by the study of the ancient poets. Through long-standing attachment, therefore, he devoted himself to Julian, who always makes mention of him with affectionate remembrance.

The young Prince was brought up in perfect retirement, so that he excited no suspicion, and remained at a distance from the burthensome ceremonies of the court. His instructor sought to awaken in him a sense of the great and the noble through the poetry of Homer, and examples taken from ancient history, and thus confirmed his mind in that direction to which also it was naturally inclined. For there was implanted in him by nature a longing after things above, that strove to mount into the heavens beyond the limits of actual life. This bias discovered itself in little but striking traits in his yet undeveloped childhood.† "From my earliest age," he said of himself, "a powerful attachment to the splendor of the God of the Sun (*Helios*) was implanted in me; the appearance of the heavenly light used to carry me so entirely out of myself, even in my childhood, that I not only strove to look upon it with a steady eye, but often went out into the open air on bright, cloudless nights, and, careless of aught else, I gazed in admiration on the beauty of the starry heavens, without thinking of myself, without hearing what was said to me; so that I was already often taken

* See his *Hymn. in solem.* p. 130. See APPENDIX IX.

for an astrologer before my beard was grown, and yet no book upon the subject had ever fallen in my way; nay, I did not even know what the term meant. But I could say much more than this, if I attempted to relate how at such times I thought of the *gods*."

A person of Julian's powerful and elevated mind could not be made torpid either from the depressing and confined position in which he lived since his earliest childhood, or from the constant dangers from which he had hitherto been saved, as it were, by accident. His longing after liberty and his pursuit of the extraordinary must have been the more excited by the contrast of his life with the bias of his disposition; the same may be said of the inclination which had arisen within him, of seeking out of the realities of life what he could not find within it. Great pains were taken to bring him up in the Christian faith, and to guard him from the contagion of heathenism. With this view he was not allowed to attend the rhetoric school of Libanius, who had just commenced teaching at Constantinople, and was in the highest reputation.* Another rhetorician of less ability was appointed as his instructor; a man who, though in his heart inclined to heathenism, maintained the appearance of being a zealous Christian, and thereby gained the favor of the emperor.

About the year of our Lord 344, when Julian was

* Compare Liban. *Panegyr. et Orat. de vitâ suâ.*

now in his thirteenth year, the suspicious Constantius removed him and his brother Gallus (who soon after the death of Constantine had sought for safety in flight) to one of his estates, called Macellum, in the remote and mountainous province of Cappadocia. In this place they lived together for six years,* in a state, as Julian has described it, of splendid slavery, guarded on all sides and surrounded by persons who strove to bring them up in humble obedience to the emperor. Indeed, great pains were taken to reconcile them to him; they were often assured that he had been induced, against his will, to consent to the murder of their relations, partly from having been deceived, and partly through the violence of his riotous troops; that he regretted the deed, and looked upon his childless state, as well as his ill success in the Persian war, as a punishment for his crime. This statement might really have been well grounded, and this momentary contrition might probably have procured better treatment for the two brothers.

Meanwhile the young princes were watched by ecclesiastics, who endeavored to fix them in the Christian faith; but probably they were not themselves thoroughly imbued with the true spirit of Christianity; for men of this sort were not to be found in the service of the court. As Julian had by nature a strong bias towards heavenly things, and eagerly followed all

* See Appendix X.

the impressions that were made upon his youthful mind, he now became zealous for the Christian worship, and abhorred heathenism. The reverence at that time generally paid to martyrs had perhaps something in it which flattered his fancy; he conducted himself as their devout admirer; he engaged, in emulation of his brother, in the labor of erecting a chapel over the grave of a martyr, whose memory was there honored: he frequently attended the churches, and even held the appointment of a reader* of the Holy Scriptures. His love for the old Greek poets, and for the Greek literature in general, still continued; andin Cappadocia (where the school of Origen, which he - that literature in the highest esteem, was the prevailing theological party) he could easily find means, even through the Christian clergy, of gratifying his inclination. He procured Greek books for transcription, from the well-filled library of George† of Cappadocia, who had been forcibly installed by the Arian party as Bishop of Alexandria in place of St. Athanasius.‡

At the end of this six-year's residence in Cappadocia both the brothers were recalled to Constantinople by the emperor, whose suspicions were for some time appeased. Gallus was introduced at court, and Julian, having obtained permission to follow his inclination, attended with great diligence the schools of the

* Lector, or Anagnostes.

† The tutelar saint of England.

‡ See Socrates, ii. 14.

Greek literature, and courted the society of the most celebrated scholars who then resided there.* Niocles,† a Lacedæmonian jurist, a friend of Libanius, and well acquainted with the ancient philosophy, explained to him Homer and the other old poets. The philosophical, allegorical mode of exposition was well adapted to excite Julian's ardent imagination, and stimulate his mind in the investigation of hidden truth. His enthusiasm and talents collected so many persons about him, that the suspicion of the emperor, who was on the point of leaving Constantinople in order to march an army westward against Magnentius, was excited afresh. Not thinking it safe therefore to leave him alone in Constantinople, he sent him to Nicomedia in Bithynia, a city of less notoriety, but a flourishing seat of learning, that he might there follow up his inclination for study.

About this time (A. D. 351) the emperor advanced Gallus, Julian's brother, to the rank of Cæsar. In the meanwhile, Libanius, the enthusiastic supporter of the new Platonic ideas of religion, had been expelled from Constantinople by his enemies among the Sophists of the place, and at length entered into the service of the city of Nicomedia. Julian, before his departure from Constantinople, had promised his Christian instructors upon his oath never to attend the lectures of this man,

* See Julian, *Ep.* 9, p. 377.

† See Socrat. *loc. cit.*—Libanius (*Legat. ad Julian*) says of him, εἴδως, εἴπερ τις, τῆς Ὁμήρου γνώμης τὰ ἀπόῤῥητα.

whose influence upon his religious views was so much dreaded; a prohibition which was calculated to excite a distrust in Christianity in the mind of the ardent youth, as well as the greater desire to become acquainted with these dreaded expositions, and such formidable eloquence. He certainly kept faithfully to his promise, yet at a considerable expense he caused the daily lectures and discourses of the philosopher to be secretly conveyed to him in Nicomedia, studied them with great industry, and endeavored to model himself in the art of speaking by that pattern. Hence originated his steady attachment to Libanius, and also the report that he had been his scholar.*

Up to this time Julian's devotion to Christianity† was not mere simulation;‡ yet, probably, from his constant study of the ancient poetry and history of Greece, and the natural activity of his mind, a longing had arisen for a religion which was better adapted to the ardor of his imagination, and afforded more occupation for his speculative bias. The theological controversies then prevailing were certainly far from recommending Christianity to a mind like his, nor could a religion that revealed the Godhead in the form of a servant, attract a heart that was devoted to the great, the extraordinary, and the showy. While he was in this sort of temperature he heard some philoso-

* See Libanius, *Legat. ad Julian.*

† He was now 20 years old.—*T.*

‡ See APPENDIX XI.

phers discourse "concerning the origin and the nature of the soul, its imprisonment and its liberation; how it was brought down to the earth, and by what means it could be raised again; as also concerning the nature and operations of gods and demons." What doctrine could have had more charms for Julian than that the soul, derived from higher regions, was imprisoned in the body as in a dungeon, and was set free from the bands of matter by the kind assistance of the gods, the authors of all that was great and exalted in human ordinances, and who evidently revealed themselves in their salutary influence upon men's souls and bodies?

He now soon learnt how to interpret the dark surmises of his soul, as, from his early youth, he had directed his eyes with a sort of longing to the sun; he felt that the god, Helios, to whom his soul belonged, the god who connected the visible with the invisible world, had drawn him thither. He found here glittering symbols, rich materials for his ardent and profound imagination; and mysteries, which did not, like those of Christianity, set limits to his speculations, but found ample occupation for his mind and spirit in the task of symbolical interpretation. He met not here with suffering saints who had wrought nothing great or remarkable in the world, but heroes who had displayed extraordinary feats of strength, and whose example kindled in him a desire for great exploits. From the reputation already gained by Julian many learned men and philosophers were induced to visit Nicomedia, to see the youth through whom they hoped for the restoration of the ancient worship of the gods, and to confirm him still more in the faith to which he was already so well inclined.

The individual who made the greatest impression on Julian was the philosopher Maximus,* whose philosophy was interwoven with theosophy and demonology. He was a man who sought what was showy and extraordinary, who eagerly searched into futurity, and was given to the practice of magic. He was exactly the person to exercise the greatest influence on the ardent disposition of the Prince, struggling as it already was to pass beyond the limits of this confined existence. Predictions, for which the then state of society naturally afforded occasion, had been widely spread among the heathen, that Christianity was soon about to fall, and that a restorer of the ancient religion should rule over the Roman empire. This of course was made to point at Julian. The wonderful instances of providential care through which he had been hitherto preserved in his struggle with dangers and difficulties, connected, as they now were, with these prophecies, raised in him the strongest conviction that he had been expressly sent into the world by the gods to raise up again by their restored worship the empire that had fallen away through the contempt shown to the religion of his father-land.

* See Appendix XII.

His recent mode of life caused him to give a more lively reception to this conviction, so that he henceforth viewed all events that befell him in this feeling and belief. From this period he became an enthusiastic admirer of Polytheism, and made use of the Christian religion (to which he had before earnestly attached himself) only as a mask wherewith to conceal his real opinions. Maximus, who himself had come to him from Ephesus, induced him, probably by the representation he gave him of the assemblage of philosophers in Ionia, to go thither.* He previously obtained the emperor's permission, who indeed gladly saw him drawn off by scientific pursuits from engaging in political schemes. His enthusiasm on these subjects was there raised still higher by the most distinguished philosophers of the age, in whose system philosophy was completely amalgamated with the symbols of Polytheism. The theosophist Chrysanthius contributed most to this, who sought to lead the mind of Julian from the showy† promises of magic to profounder notions of philosophy, and thereby to moderate the impetuosity of his nature. "He withdrew me (said Julian at a later period) from all that was passionate and irregular, and endeavored to make me sober-

* Ammianus, 15, 2; Gregory Naz. *Orat.* i. *Stilit;* Liban. *Legat ad Julian,* p. 175; Sozom. v. 2, and the letter of Gallus to Julian, testify to this journey of Julian to Asia Minor, and especially to Ionia.

† That Julian did not love mere show, like Maximus, and was in general of a soberer cast, was proved by his subsequent proceedings.

minded; he taught me above all things to exercise virtue, and to consider the gods as the sources of all good."

The rumor of Julian's sentiments rapidly spread among the heathens, who formed new hopes, collected more predictions, and privately sacrificed and prayed to the gods for his preservation. Even his brother Gallus, who was staying in the neighboring parts of Asia, was disturbed by the report; until the ecclesiastic Aëtius* brought him intelligence that he (Julian) still frequently attended the churches, and showed himself a zealous worshipper at the tombs of the martyrs. Gallus upon this exhorted him earnestly to remain true to the Christian faith.† After Julian had thus enjoyed the privilege of living agreeably to his own inclinations for about four years, this pleasure was again disturbed by an event of a most painful kind. His only remaining brother, Gallus, (who had

* This Aëtius was originally a physician at Antioch; during the Arian controversies he applied the Dialectics of Aristotle, and the Categories in particular, to the doctrine of Christ's Godhead, and from thence concluded that Christ was not truly God, because nothing could exist between God and that which was created. He gained the friendship of Gallus, who resided at Antioch, and through his patronage he became deacon; but after the murder of Gallus he was, on a charge of heresy as well as his connection with him, deposed and banished. Julian, who had esteemed and loved him, partly as his brother's friend, partly as his own, and partly also as a learned man (for Aëtius was familiar with the Aristotelic philosophy), now treated him with more respect than any other ecclesiastic. See Julian. *Epist.* 31, Book v. and Sozom. iii. 15; iv. 24; v. 5.

† See *Epist.* 64.

indeed by his violent* temper made himself many enemies, and excited many suspicions against himself,) was taken from him, A. D. 354, by him who had already shed the blood of so many of his relations, and who extended the same suspicious spirit to Julian also with many other persons connected with Gallus.

From his journey from Nicomedia into Ionia, his brother's neighborhood, the emperor conceived a suspicion of a secret understanding between them.† He was conducted, under strict guard, from Ionia to Italy,

* This is much too lenient a statement of the conduct and character of the weak and cruel Gallus, urged on as he was by his wife Constantina, who (as Gibbon says) is described not as a woman but as an infernal fury.—*T.*

† We may draw this conclusion by comparing Ammianus *loc. cit.*; Julian's *Epist. ad Athen.*; and Libanius *in Juliani necem.* Julian's epistle is a special authority for this part of his biography. See his *Works*, p. 272, for his seven months' *surveillance*, six of which he spent at Milan, in the same city with the Emperor; his departure thence for Ionia, p. 273; his recall from thence, p. 274; his removal to Greece, thence again to Milan, where he for the first time met with Eusebia. The context proves that the relation of his dream and his determination to commit every thing to the gods, belongs to this period; for it is clearly his aim to relate how he had strength given him to endure the trial of living with the murderer of his brother, *e. g.* ἐνταῦθα χρὴ μὴ παραλείπειν, πῶς ἐιλόμην, κ. τ. λ. p. 274. This leads him to speak of his sufferings on that account and his prayer to the gods. He then returns to the intention of his narrative, viz. the means by which he obtained strength to accommodate himself to all that befell him. That narrative begins thus, συνέβη δὲ τι καὶ τοιοῦτον. Ammianus is not very exact here (neither indeed did his proposed object require it of him): he does not distinguish between Julian's first and second journey to Greece, and he speaks of the latter as having happened before the murder of Silvanus, which yet, according to Julian's own testimony, preceded his second journey to Greece; since it was not till after he had come to Milan that Constantius, after the death of Silvanus, arrived there.

where Constantius then resided, and he spent seven months in a state of the greatest anxiety. Closely watched on all sides, and seeing death every moment impending over him, he was at length delivered from this oppressive imprisonment by the good services of the empress Eusebia, who was favorably inclined towards him, and obtained permission for him to return to his maternal estates in Ionia. The emperor, however, who since the insurrection of Silvanus had become more jealously watchful, discovered a new cause of suspicion: he recalled him therefore a second time, but gave him permission, when he had now got as far as Greece, to withdraw himself for a time to Athens.* Here, in the society of the philosophers, priests, and students, who were still assembled at the ancient seat of knowledge, he forgot all his misfortunes; and here his spirit found that freedom, which the relations of life did not afford him, in his efforts after the godlike and in the friendship of the gods, who always became so much the more his friends, the more he felt himself to be deserted by men.

An imperial order however soon called him away again from this peaceful abode to the emperor and to Milan. With burning tears he left a city that had become so dear to him, to go probably to encounter death. He raised his hands in prayer to the consecrated cit-

* This was probably done because he was himself occupied by the commotions excited by Silvanus.

adel of Minerva, and besought her to protect her devoted servant, and not betray him or allow him to die even in Athens. And he evidently believed that he experienced her protection throughout life, and that she was ever with him and delivered him from all the critical circumstances in which he afterwards found himself. On his arrival at Milan the emperor was absent in consequence of the insurrection of Silvanus; but the empress, Eusebia, sent many friendly messages to him through one of her eunuchs, and hinted to him that he need only transmit to her in confidence a written statement of his wishes. Tired out with the oppressive anxiety of his position, he wrote a letter, in which he begged and adjured her to get him permission to return home as soon as possible. It occurred to him however afterwards, how dangerous it might be for him to write a letter to the empress; and, doubting what he ought to do, he begged of the gods to reveal to him that night whether he should send the letter or not. He was assured in a dream, that in case he did so a most cruel death awaited him. He therefore withheld the letter, and determined, from that moment, to render himself without fear or anxiety to the gods; since man (he said to himself) surveys only the present moment, but the wisdom of the gods, on the contrary, surveys all things; and they alone can reveal to men as well as bring to pass, always what is best. "Thou art ready (said he again to himself) to flatter and do homage out of the fear of death, when thou mayest throw off all trouble from thyself, and transfer all care for thee to the gods." He determined therefore to follow his own notions of duty as well as he could, but to resign his fate wholly to the gods; to strive after nothing in the world as a matter of anxiety, but to receive with confidence what they were pleased to grant to him. With this feeling of pious resignation to the Divine Will, he submitted (painful as it was to the feelings of his heart) to dwell under the same roof with the murderer of his nearest relations, when the emperor, whose snare seemed to threaten him with death, summoned him to the palace, on his return from the murder of Silvanus.

At length, through the entreaties of Eusebia, he was released from the fetters of a life at court, a life so repulsive to his free and noble spirit that hated every thing that was effeminate, and he obtained permission to return to his beloved Athens. Here he once more lived, engaged in the study of ancient science and art, and the rites of the ancient religion. He was initiated in the Eleusinian mysteries, and formed connections with young men who were studying Greek literature there with him, some of whom afterwards went over from those studies to that of theology, and became distinguished teachers in the Christian church, as Basil of Cæsarea and Gregory* of Nazianzus. The

* I have ventured here to read *Gregorius* instead of *Georgius*, as it is in the original.—*T.*

latter* even then remarked in Julian that enthusiasm for the polytheistic religion, which, though he endeavored to conceal it, expressed itself in all that he did.

When he had now spent several months so agreeably to his own inclination, he was (A. D. 356, æt. 25) recalled by the emperor, much against his will; and he reluctantly sacrificed his liberty to a station of honor through which he was drawn again into a species of captivity. Constantius, who wanted help under the simultaneous pressure of the Persian and Gallic wars, nominated him to the dignity of Cæsar, on the advice of Eusebia, who was partially inclined towards Julian. He could now even far less than in his former private life, venture to practise openly the worship of the gods of Greece, since he was still carefully watched on all sides, and his connection with the heathen party was still more dreaded. Still in the midst of his unsettled life among the rude Gallic nations and the wars with which he was occupied, he continued to study with the same enthusiasm the works of the ancient philosophers and poets, and (what was in his opinion completely connected therewith) the mysteries of the old religion; nay, in his mode of life he followed its regulations wherever he could with safety, although he still concealed his real sentiments under a show of Christianity, and disclosed his genuine opinions only to a chosen few whose ideas agreed with his own, and on whose fidelity he could rely. The first person who

* *Orat. Stel.* ii.

entered into his religious views and encouraged him in this polytheistic worship was only a trusty servant, though probably of a cultivated mind and a scholar, as he was the superintendent of his library. The next was an official person whom the emperor had placed near him as his adviser for the purpose of watching his movements. This person, however, in opposition to that intention, became his devoted adherent, being bound to him by the closest friendship that sprung from similar modes of thinking, especially on religious subjects. He therefore incurred the suspicions of the emperor, and was soon recalled. Julian was intimately connected also with other Greek philosophers and scholars, as well as the physician Oribasius,* who sought for indications of the future in predictions both old and new, as well as by auspices, and endeavored to encourage and cheer him under critical circumstances.

His nights were divided between the affairs of state and his studies. As soon as he arose, before he proceeded to the examination of public business, he prayed

* See Julian's *Epist. ad Athen.* p. 277.—By means of those felicitous predictions of Oribasius a report was widely circulated among the heathen that he was the means of elevating Julian to the imperial throne. See Eunapius, *Vit. Oribasii.* That Sallust was devoted to heathenism we learn from Socrates, iii. 19. "Not without the favor of the Muses (says Julian in his consolatory address to Sallust, *Orat.* 8) have we often sung together of the plastic power, the justice, and the intellect which conducts the transitory affairs of men." He also dedicated to him, at a later time, several of his treatises on religious subjects, with a view of making him acquainted with the mysteries of theology. See *Orat.* iv. *de Sole.* p. 157.

to Mercury, as the all-pervading* mind that spreads every where and fosters the seed of life, and connects the things of eternity with those of time. The happy results, however, of his enterprises in Gaul excited afresh the suspicion of the emperor, who thought he could no longer in safety leave to his disposal so large a force as that with which he had effected so much; he therefore, A. D. 360, recalled from him the greater part of his troops. This order, however, was received by the army, then assembled at Paris, with universal displeasure, and the soldiers with loud clamor surrounded the palace of the young Cæsar. He, who had formed a resolution to follow in all things the guidance of the gods, fell upon his knees and prayed to Jupiter that he would point out to him by an omen which way he should proceed. When he thought he had discovered the expected sign he was still undecided, till he was compelled by the army to accept the imperial throne, and was proclaimed by the title of Augustus.

Not yet, however, fully determined, and musing

* Ammian. 16, 4. Occulte Mercurium supplicabat, quem mundi *velociorem* sensum esse, motum mentium suscitantem, theologicæ prodidere doctrinæ. Mercury (as quoted by Eusebius, *Præpar. Evangel.* iii. 2) is explained by Porphyry to be the all-creating, truth-revealing mind. Ὁ λόγος πάντων ποιητικὸς καὶ ἑρμηνευτικός. Jamblichus, *de Myster.* c. 1, calls Mercury the god who is the common creative director of all human reason, from whom all our knowledge of divine things proceeds, wherever it exists among men. It was therefore natural that the Christian teachers found therein an analogy to Christ as the Λόγος in whom the Deity was revealed. So Justin, *Apolog.* ii. compares Christ as the Λόγος, the begotten Son of God, with Mercury as the Λόγος παρὰ Θεοῦ ἀγγελτικός.

over his plan of proceeding, he spent the winter at Vienne in Gaul; prophecies and dreams inspired him with still greater hopes, yet he thought himself obliged, in his uncertain position, to conceal his actual opinions, that he might not alienate from him the powerful Christian party. With this view he attended the Christian churches on the festival of the Epiphany, the 6th of January. To the messengers of the emperor, who promised him life and personal security, he expressed* his sentiments by replying, "It was better for him to intrust the care of his life to the gods than to the sword of Constantius." As he returned (A. D. 361) from Gaul towards Constantinople, he made his religious opinions more known upon his march, especially in the cities of Greece, which still contained many adherents of the ancient religion. In his dearly-beloved Athens he caused the hitherto closed temples of Minerva and the other gods and goddesses to be again opened; and there, for the first time, he publicly practised the heathen worship, and called upon all other persons to follow his example in honoring the gods.

In order to show his recognition of the Athenians as the ancient model of righteous judges (before whose tribunal even gods had been wont to appear), he addressed to them an epistle containing an account of his whole life and conduct. The restoration of the

* See Zosim. L. iii. c. 9.

ancient worship was considered by him of such impor tance, that amongst his greater undertakings for that object he took pains to settle a dispute between the old sacerdotal families in Athens, (in which all the heathen persuasion took a part,) that the peaceable worship of the gods might not be disturbed thereby. Before he left the city he asked counsel of the gods by sacrifice; nor did he set out upon his march before all the omens appeared propitious to him; and with similar anxiety he now sought on all occasions to acquaint himself by the usual means with the events of the yet distant future.

In the midst of these preparations he received the unexpected intelligence* of the death of the emperor Constantius. The news was so unlooked for by all, that no one at first believed it, though Julian referred them to predictions which had already announced it.†

* Julian, in his 17th Epistle, addressed to Oribasius, finds the predictions of that individual to be confirmed by his dream:—"I thought I saw a lofty tree growing in a very large saloon. The tree was bent down to the ground, and close to its roots another smaller and much more vigorous plant shot up. I felt great anxiety lest some one should tear away this smaller with the larger tree; and as I drew near, I perceived the lofty one stretched upon the ground, but the little one standing erect and rising towards heaven. On seeing this, I said in distress, What a tree was that! it is to be feared that the sapling cannot have escaped unscathed by its fall. But an unknown voice said to me, Take but a closer view, and be of good courage, for the root is still left in the earth, so that the young tree remains unhurt and will stand so much the firmer."

† See Libanius, *in nec. Julian.* p. 289. It was, however, a feature

His belief that he was under the special guidance of the gods, and that they had made him ruler of the Roman empire in order to re-establish their former worship, became now still more powerful; so also did his determination to bring back again the old customs, regulations, and religious ceremonies through which the Greeks and Romans had become the greatest nations of the world. Soon after his entrance into Constantinople (a city, which ever since its revival by the first Christian emperor, had been the seat of Christianity) he ordered the temples there to be thrown

in the character of Julian (and one which originated in the elevation of his sentiments) that he by no means suffered himself to be alarmed by auspices or omens when he wished to carry any thing into execution; and that he knew how to give a favorable turn to them, with rapid presence of mind, when they had been unfavorably reported by others. For instance, as he was exercising himself at Paris, in a variety of movements with his shield on his arm, the shield was so completely broken that the handle only remained in his grasp; this he held firm in his hand, and, while all the bystanders were frightened at the omen, he coolly said, "Let no one fear, for I still hold fast what I held before." See Ammian. 21, 2. In the same manner he acted also in the last Persian war, when the soothsayers endeavored in vain to restrain him. In the conviction that a higher kind of wisdom was with the gods, and in a consciousness that he exercised his power under their control, he waited for no oracle from above, and spent not the time for action in compliance with the lazy movements of the soothsayers, but was himself his own Pythia. Liban. *Panegyr. Julian.* p. 183. In this he displayed the truth of his religious impressions, distinct from servile superstition; since he sought to realize the notions which animated him, and fulfilled his mission with a devotion to the will of the gods, to whose wisdom he confidently resigned the final issue.

open, and himself offered to the genius of Rome* a sacrifice of thanksgiving for the great good fortune which he had bestowed upon him.

* Socrat. iii. 11.

SECTION III.

JULIAN'S VIEW OF RELIGION AND PHILOSOPHY IN GENERAL; HIS VIEW OF CHRISTIANITY RESULTING THEREFROM; AND THE MEANS BY WHICH HE ENDEAVORED, AS EMPEROR, TO REALIZE HIS RELIGIOUS IDEAS.

THE different and contradictory views and representations of Julian's behavior towards the Christians have arisen in part from the fact, that his actions have been considered nakedly by themselves, and not as they proceeded from his religious mode of thinking. In attempting to exhibit them fairly, we must turn back our attention to the preceding introductory Section; since the religious view of Julian's character can only be understood by studying the spirit in which the *later* heathenism opposed itself to Christianity. His theology indeed was formed by the efforts then made to connect the revelation of God in the soul of man with the old traditions and myths as well as the ancient worship of their fathers; to give the latter a living spirit by means of the former; to unite the former, by means of the latter, to something firm and independent of human authority, as being hallowed by its remote antiquity; and, with the view of giving the system an objective, universal adaptation for the nations, to attach it to a form that would operate upon all by exciting and elevating their religious impressions.

He had a lively consciousness of "the laws that are written by the gods upon the souls of men, and through which, without any further instruction, we are convinced of the existence of the Deity." From this Deity originated all those systems of philosophy that proceeded on correct notions, and they all therefore agreed with one another, because they represented precisely the same thing, though under different and, apparently, contradictory forms. "Let no one (said he) cut up philosophy into many parts, or (to express myself better) let no one make for us many philosophies out of the one and true one. One may go to Athens by different routes, by water or by land, by the highways or by the short cuts and by-roads." By the former he understood those who, like the Stoics, attached themselves to the political and practical life; by the latter, those who, like the Cynics, despised all human forms and regulations, seeking after and exercising only the truth. "Let no one (he proceeds) make it an objection against us, if some persons who followed their own peculiar paths, have lost their way or been cast on some other coast, allured by pleasure or ambition (as by Circe or the Lotophagi), and hindered from proceeding farther and reaching this, their proper haven. Let the first men only in every school be looked to, and you will find them all in harmony." (See his *Oration*, vi. p. 185.)

Whilst he went back to this inward revelation of

the Deity (through which man becomes conscious of an existence, unbroken in its duration, and preceding all distinction of time or space), he acknowledged the original unity of the Divine Being, as in fact every reflecting polytheist acknowledged it, as the one Ruler of all things and from whom all things proceed; whether he were called "the Power that lies beyond the powers and ken of human reason," or "the Archetype of all being," or "the One Being," or "the Chief Good,"—from this one Cause flowed all beauty, all perfection, unity and exceeding strength. (*Oration*, iv. p. 152.)

He who has arrived at a consciousness of this one existence, apprehends at the same time that there is implanted in man a longing after the same, or an instinctive desire of immortality. And this immortality consists not merely in a progressive transplanting of the individual being into an altered or *metamorphosed* state, but in being raised to an existence really and for the first time independent; an existence elevated above all change and accidents of external forms, whose image and idea we bear impressed in our inner man, combined with that of our real personality. The *untaught* polytheist, recognizing his personality solely in its temporal manifestation, looks upon the natural life as man's only real existence, and the realms of the dead as an empty dream, the mere striving and longing after the lost reality; just as the philosophy which has been *refined* by the contrary process in the scale of education, removes the opposition between heaven and earth, to which all human witnesses testify, and declares the belief in a continued personal existence to be but an egotistic conceit. And this it does, because it recognizes that personality only as it discloses itself, broken, limited, and restrained by the relations of time; not as it reveals itself, by and for itself, in man's inner nature, reposing upon and hidden in the Deity, of whom it is itself a faint conception, allowing itself to be known only *in part*, as *through a glass darkly.*

"The soul (says Julian) will then require no farther growth or progressive improvement, being no more subject to changes of form, but raised into a higher region of existence, the pure spiritual world." (*Orat.* iv. p. 136.) He prays (*ibid.* page 138), "that God would raise him after death to the calm *freedom* of the Divine life, and deliver him from the law of *necessity* to which all *temporal* concerns are subject." The reflecting polytheist, however, is distinguished from the monotheist not so much by the fact, that he does not acknowledge the unity of the Divine nature, as in these respects:—that he does not practically allow the Deity any influence upon life, or refer life's varying circumstances thereto; that he does not look upon the connection between God and man to be of a direct, immediate kind, but (separating the Divine and the natural principle from each other) he connects and fills up the interval between them by a series of Divine beings; and, lastly, that he distributes and divides what the monotheist comprises in his idea of the Godhead, by making it an object for the imagination in many different ways and by means of actual personifications.

Julian considered the first and highest object of worship to be the Incomprehensible, Divine Being, the everlasting Source of Good, which, as it were by a multiplication of its own essence, generates from itself Divine* beings, which form the first scale of existence, and are entirely† distinct from all that is merely natural and temporal. Next in the scale come the executive deities, unconfined by space or time, who govern and control the natural world;‡ and these operate directly upon the material, perishable world by means of their ever-living representatives, the stars, which so well exhibit and communicate their influence. In this manner the operation of the Divine life was extended from the highest in the scale of being, through the different intermediate members, to the very lowest. That

* The passage in Plato (*De Rep.* L. vi. p. 116, ed. Bib.,) in which he compares the operation of the sun with that of the Supreme Good in the spiritual world, was turned to account by the speculative imagination of this age. This idea, that the First in the scale of existence gives copies of himself, though differently expressed, in the lower gradations of being, is exhibited in the poetico-philosophical systems which were formed after the birth of Christ.

† The Θεοὶ νοήτοι, *Orat.* 9, p. 139.

‡ Θεοὶ νόεροι.

which the Eternal Good was to the first in the scale of being (that Eternal Good, which originates all life and sustains it by a common bond of union), *Helios*, the god of the sun, the revealed emblem of the Supreme Good, is to the second scale of beings. In a similar manner he communicates his power and influence to those beings, he connects them mutually with himself, as their common centre, and through the higher gradations of being, into one great whole. Again, the visible sun is the image and revelation of the same original in that visible part of the universe which is raised above this scene of change and decay; it there stands in the same relation to the other heavenly bodies; imparts life and strength to them as revelations of the other gods; connects all those revelations with their eternal Archetype, and, as the common centre of the whole as well as the conveyer of good to every grade of existence, extends their combined influence to the whole material world.

The One great Cause of all being (he says, *ibid.* p. 132) produced, together with the other operative immaterial causes (from himself and entirely like himself), the great god Helios; and what the Supreme Good does amongst the highest gods, the latter does amongst those spiritual beings. The former produces among them existence, beauty, unity and perfection; all this the god Helios effects in the succeeding grade of being. The third power is that visible, shining body, which is the source of support and health to the visible world. (See *ibid.* p. 133.) Thus in the sensible objects of the universe, above him and around him, Julian saw a representation of the being and the operations of the Most High; an idea which must have had great attractions for his thoughtful, poetic mind. "You believe" (he therefore wrote to the people of Alexandria, p. 434), "you believe that Jesus is God, whom neither your fathers nor yourselves have ever *seen;* but you believe not this of him whom from *the beginning of time* the whole human race *sees* and honors as their benefactor,—even the great Helios, the living, animated, spiritual, beneficent image of the Supreme Father, who is exalted above all the powers of reason."

In the same spirit he says (*apud Cyrill, contra Julian.* p. 65), "the stars were only called gods inasmuch as they were the representatives of the invisible gods, each one being made known to us separately, according to the peculiar nature and operation of each; and these invisible gods themselves dwelt in the essence of the Supreme Creator, from whom they were produced." Julian considered himself as living under the especial guidance of the god Helios, and his soul* (which thus revealed him to him) as appointed to connect again the fallen visible world with the Invisible, by re-establishing the worship of the gods.† With the Divine Life (according to Julian's view, and that which

* Ὀπαδὸς θεοῦ ἡλίου. † See APPENDIX IX.

has been already exhibited in the characteristics of this polytheistic philosophy) is also necessarily connected the entire revelation and development of the same, down to the lowest material forms, (beyond which there remains nothing but the bare boundary-line of being,) that is, matter* in and by itself; in other words, the whole internal and external creation; thus connecting the ever-existing, self-subsisting Godhead with nature in its state of constant progression and growth.

With such views, then, the Christian doctrine of the creation, dated from a commencement of time, must have appeared to him as something desolate, and void, and completely unphilosophical. Indeed he looked upon it as a kind of anthropomorphism, to apply the idea of a beginning, or any reference to time, to the operations of the gods. "It is not without some risk, (he said, in his *Orat.* iv. p. 146), even with the view only of making the matter more intelligible, that we speak of an incipient creation of the universe; since the god Helios, from all eternity, produced the visible from the unseen world, without relation to time,† and by his divine will." This universe (he says, *ibid.* p. 131) existed from eternity, without any temporal beginning, as it also endures to all eternity." He made the peculiarity of the myths to consist in this,

* *τὸ τῆς στερησέως ὄνομα μετὰ ἀμύδρας ἐπινοίας*—*Orat.* v. p. 161.

* 'Εν τῷ νυν—in the actual *now*—as he expresses it, in order to show hat all idea of temporal progression must be removed from the notion.

that they represented as having happened at a definite point of time what was grounded in the eternal laws of things.* Agreeably to this view, it seemed to him a proof of superstition and unphilosophic ignorance in the Christians, when they taught that God created all things, heaven and earth alike, generally and individually, out of nothing; and, moreover, that he has doomed the whole material universe to destruction. For (he reasoned) the causes of all things were eternally based in the Divine Nature; although the causes of imperishable things, abiding as they do in everlasting existence, differ in their nature from the ever-enduring causes of perishable things, from which a never-ending succession of being is produced. (*Orat.* vi. p. 185.) Effects differing in kind could not originate from similar causes; the whole being eternal and unchangeable, shows itself thereby to be the work of the Universal Creator; but the individual, perishable, material beings could not be derived from the same Creator, but were the productions of the individual gods.†

The monotheist forms an ideal conception of human nature as being the image of God; he therefore looks upon the whole human race, proceeding from one man, as a manifestation of the unity of the Godhead. The polytheist, on the contrary, conceives there are various living ideals in the various gods,

* *Orat.* v. p. 171.

† See Cyrill. *cant. Julian,* L. ii. p. 65.

who, in a way corresponding with their nature, make themselves known through the characters of men destined to express an image and likeness of them. Julian, therefore, rejected the notion that the whole human race was descended from one common parent, and considered it more probable that the different gods, receiving the immortal souls from the Creator, formed simultaneously many individual men, progenitors of the various nations; and that the marked difference of manners and institutions in different countries attests the truth of this theory.* Undoubtedly (he argued) all would be *one and complete* in the *common Father and Ruler of all;* but he could not reveal himself in his oneness and completeness in the work of *creation.* Amidst the *divided* and *individual* acts, one or other power, and one or another god would predominate, and so every nation would be placed under a different god,† whose leading character it would exhibit in its daily life, as the source from whence, in accordance with that character, its peculiar institutions and laws proceeded. It is not enough here to say, as the Christians are accustomed, that the difference in nations exists only because God has so commanded it, since the commands of God are not, like the commands of men, of a perishable or transitory character; but as he himself is everlasting, so the natural qualities and laws of existence would be eternal and indestructible. The

* Fragment *Ep. ad Lacerd.* p. 292.

† Θεὸς ἐθνάρχης.

destined character therefore of nations, and their modes of life, reached a point beyond which they could not advance; and their several lawgivers added but little, by means of education, to the natural abilities of men. Indeed, as long as the *Roman Empire* endures, no western people will easily be found that is devoted to the sciences; the *cleverest* of them as yet having never got beyond the *rhetorical* art.*

[Julian did not perceive that in using such language he was bearing witness to the Divine power of the religion against which he wrote; for we now see that it alone has effected, and that it alone could effect, what Greek and Roman science and culture were not equal to. Before the times of Christianity, each nation knew not only religion but also science, art, and accomplishments, only after its own peculiar views, and in a form interwoven with its national *characteristics* and *relations*. But how could the education of Greece and Rome be ingrafted upon a foreign nation, entirely different in its character, without that nation thereby losing its self-dependence, and therefore becoming weak and spiritless? Generally, indeed, that education must be shallow and superficial which is opposed to the course of nature, according to which there must first be the fresh juice of life, which makes the young plant shoot upwards, and then in their proper course produces the leaf, and the bud,

* *Ap. Cyrill. c. Julian.* L. iii.

and last of all, the fruit. This animal juice, or sap, for the human plant, man, is religion, which alone (as history proves) can draw him up from the slime of earth. Thus it was that Christianity civilized the nations which appeared to the Romans incapable of culture; it first of all stirred up religious and moral susceptibilities by simple annunciations, intelligible to the hearts of all men; and these powers thus excited could not but awaken all other seeds of life, to be cultivated after the peculiar fashion of the nation. No zeal for science, however, no admiration of ethics or philosophy, whether Stoic or even Platonic, could induce men to abandon the seat of learning and civilization, for the purpose of instructing perfectly barbarous nations. Nothing could bring men to do this, but a religion which announced to men that He who had redeemed them from misery had come down from heaven itself, and that One had given his life for all, in order that all might have an equal claim to the enjoyment of the highest of all blessings.]

From this idea (of national character dependent on different gods) Julian deduced the sanctity and inviolability of the ancient religious institutions and traditions. "I eschew (he writes to the chief priest, Theodorus, *Ep*. 65, p. 452) a taste for innovation in every thing; especially in every thing which concerns the gods. I am convinced that we are bound to observe in every thing the original institutions and laws of our country, since it is clear that it is the gods who gave them; they could not be so excellent had they originated simply from men. We must follow no man, but only the gods; since on such matters men can only *conjecture*, while the gods necessarily *know*[*] what is true."—" Some persons"(he said,[†] speaking of an ancient legend) " who are wise in their own conceits may choose to call this an old wives' story; but I consider it better, on such a point, to adopt the belief of ancient cities, than the teaching of distinguished men of the present day, whose understanding certainly reasons ingeniously, but can attain to no sound and genuine insight." These old traditions delivered the most exalted divine doctrines in a mythological dress, since the hidden nature of the gods permits not itself to be exhibited unveiled to impure minds.

The fathers of the human race, who first explored and investigated the origin of things under the guidance of the gods, concealed their discoveries, for that very reason, under a variety of accounts. They represented that which was really founded on the eternal law of things, as something that had occurred since the beginning of time. And this they did, that the ignorant multitude might thus receive the benefit that is effected by the mere symbols unaided by the powers

* He here rested the belief in immortality on the teaching of the gods.

† *Orat.* v. p. 161.

of reason;* whilst, on the contrary, men† of talent would be induced, by what was striking or even contradictory in the myths, to suspect a higher hidden meaning, and to engage in an investigation thereof. And since man could not arrive at a knowledge of this higher truth without especial activity and sagacity, he was obliged to seek for it, not by a devout attention to, or faith in, some extraordinary opinion,‡ but by the active *working of his own mind*.§

* They ascribed, for instance, to these myths a sort of magic power of introducing the direct agency of the gods, though unseen by men, and thereby healing both mental and bodily diseases.

† Origen made use of this method for the explanation of the Bible, especially of the Old Testament. "God," he says, "has placed here and there, in the law and the historical parts, as it were *σκάνδαλα καὶ προσκόμματα καὶ ἀδύνατα*, in order that men of ability may be stimulated to the investigation of the hidden, higher sense." (See Π. ἀρχ. L. iv.) It has fared with the knowledge of the Bible, as it has with the contemplation of the universe. The ancient observers of its structure, filled with the Divine Mind which animates the universe, saw every where the immediate agency of God only, overlooking the natural causes and their operations; whilst later inquirers, who had studied and explored the latter, wished to explain every thing thereby, saw nowhere the operation of the Divine Mind, but every where only the working of machinery. Just so, the teachers of the earliest Christian era, being filled with the spirit of the Bible, followed that only on all occasions, and neglecting the natural, literal sense, began to allegorize every thing; while later students, who examined and understood the literal sense, wished to estimate every thing by that standard, not searching for the Divine Spirit with which the Scriptures are instinct, and without which the Bible is a book locked up.

‡ Julian probably made this remark in opposition to the unphilosophic faith which was commonly imputed to the Christians.

§ *Orat.* v. p. 170.—See APPENDIX XIII.

That the contradictory* and obscure is exactly the most profitable, inasmuch as it denies the power of finding relief in the natural sense, and so drives men to seek for the higher hidden sense, he thus shows in his comparison of the myths of Bacchus and Hercules. "Many persons, without paying much attention to the case, believed that Hercules was raised to Olympus by his father Jupiter, on account of his heroic virtue; and that Bacchus also, of mortal birth, was admitted to the number of the gods in consideration of his skill in theosophy and magic. Hercules however, according to the ancient legend, although from his childhood he displayed in his body an extraordinary and godlike strength, so as even to have vanquished the laws of nature, yet in a certain manner always continued within the boundaries of human nature, and allowed a certain resemblance thereto to be recognized. It was quite otherwise in the case of Bacchus; all the different features of the narrative are here in *contradiction* to the representation of a *human* nature or a *human* procreation. Here, therefore, some higher sense must be sought for, and here, truly, was found the account of a *pure God,* of his emanation from the Supreme Godhead,† and his first revelation and appearance‡ in the world. Semele, who was called his mother, was a holy priestess, who first foretold his advent; but because she could not wait with patience for the time

Απέκφαινον. † Κῦησις ἐν τοῖς νοήτοις παρὰ τῷ πὰτρι. ‡ Ἔκφανσις.

appointed in the divine will, and excited the appearance of the god too early, she was destroyed by fire at the coming of the god. (pp. 219, 221 of Julian's *Works*.)

Julian deduced the necessity of actual visible manifestations of the gods, and of a religious service addressed to the senses, from the *sensual* nature of man; and for that reason it was that the gods at first revealed themselves to the human race through their ever-living representatives, the stars. But since even to these no *sensible* honors can be paid, images were found on earth to which men could perform their worship with the hope of making the gods propitious.* These images were not however confounded with the gods themselves, for men knew well that the gods *needed* no worship.† But as subjects adopt pictures and other representations of their princes, and by paying them honor obtain their good will, though they had no necessity for such a compliment; so also in this case, the zeal which is shown in the religious service which men can pay, may well be taken as a sign of true piety. He, on the other hand, who neglects a practicable duty, under the pretence of striving after an impossibility, shows that, properly speaking, he does not strive for the latter, but only despises the former. He who

* See Appendix XIV.

† This objection might as well be made against all Divine worship, even the purest, since this can as little be said to be *necessary* to the Deity.

loves his king feels a pleasure in looking upon the king's image; he who loves his father feels the same towards his father's portrait. Just so the affectionate worshipper looks with delight upon the images of the gods, and is moved thereby to a feeling of reverence and holy awe for the invisible gods who are looking down upon him. (See Julian. *Fragment. Ep. ad Sacerdotem*, pp. 293–4.)

Julian certainly conceived an ideal standard of men, who were elevated above the different institutions of state and their religious usages; who, without allowing themselves, as citizens of the world, to be fettered with *peculiar* forms, sought only for such as are common to all men, and grounded upon their natural relation to the Deity: and who, directing their minds only to the simple, unseen truth, despised public opinion, and paid but little attention to external and symbolic worship. A nearer examination of this picture, to which at first sight Christianity might appear to correspond, shows us how little it could harmonize with Julian's mode of thinking on religious and philosophical subjects. We have here the picture of the genuine cynic sketched by Julian himself.* "This (he says, p. 187) is a philosophy of which no one can be called the founder, since it is the philosophy of nature, and common to all; and requires no peculiar systematic study. It is necessary only to will what is

* Compare *Orat.* vi. and vii. *adv. pseudo-Cynic.*

good ; provided a man strive after virtue and eschews wickedness, there is no need to read a multitude of books. This is the shortest, but it is also the most difficult way to the chief good, adapted only to a few men of extraordinary natural powers ; since the beginning of all philosophy is self-knowledge, and its end a resemblance to the gods. The true cynic, therefore, looking above all usages and opinions of men, must direct his thoughts primarily to his inner self and to God ; he should be able, as it were from the summit of Olympus, to look down upon other men, and being ever conscious that he partakes of a divine nature, should continue with a mind unshaken and immovable, in the exercise of pure and godlike thoughts."*

"Only some few, extraordinary men, however, are likely to be thus especially destined and called expressly by the Delphic god to lead other men to the knowledge of the real and the essential, and to reject all that circulates among men, as it were, in the current coin of life ; according to the oracle given to Diogenes, *παραχαράττειν τὰ νομίσματα.*† The cynic teaches more by deeds than by words ; he makes use of no images

* Pp. 225–6.

† *παραχάραξον τὸ νόμισμα*, was the oracular response given at Delphi to Diogenes the Cynic: "Mens oraculi non erat, ut Diogenes putabat, monetam esse adulterandam, sed consuetudinem sive opinionem vulgi." Kuster's note to Suidas. Or, as Suidas gives it, *τουτέστι, της τῶν πολλῶν δόξης ὑπερόρα, καὶ παράχαραττε μὴ τὴν ἀλήθειαν ἀλλὰ τὸ νόμισμα.* That is, agreeably to the primary meaning of the word, *τὸ νόμιμον ἔθος*, custom grown into a law.—*T.*

or myths, since the language of truth is simple. (p. 214.) In divine worship, also, he would care only for the essence of devotion, the pious intention. He teaches men in their acts of worship not to estimate expense more highly than piety, but the latter rather than the former, and to consider it (piety) as that without which all worship, however elaborate, all sacrifices, however numerous, would be unprofitable. (p. 214.) Diogenes did not attend the temple-worship, and showed no reverence for the altars and images of the gods, since he had nothing to offer, nor any money to purchase offerings; it was enough for him to honor the gods by the devotion of his own soul; and he considered that he gave them the highest and most precious thing he possessed, namely, his mind, which by the pious devotion of his thoughts he made a sanctuary for them." (p. 199.)

Julian thus sought to explain on these principles the well-known contempt which Diogenes expressed for the Mysteries; "In doing this he was still true to the calling to which the gods had appointed him; for as he knew that every one who would partake of the Mysteries must be a citizen of Athens, it was *this* that he despised, not the initiation in those Mysteries *on their own account*. For he looked upon himself as a citizen of the whole world, and, in the greatness of his ideas, wished for communion only with the universal nature of the gods who preside over the whole world, not those who are appropriated only to separate portions of it. Out of reverence for the gods also, he was anxious not to transgress their laws, though he trampled under foot and rejected every other claim, that he might not again be subjected to the restraint from which he rejoiced in being free. He did not, however, openly specify his true reason, but expressed himself in disparagement of the Mysteries, because he saw many persons proud of the initiation they had received, yet neglecting altogether the practice of genuine piety; he was desirous, therefore, of informing them that those men who lived a life worthy of the Mysteries, even without initiation in the same, always received a due reward from the gods; while, on the contrary, it was no advantage to the wicked, even though they had been admitted to the most holy part of the sanctuary." (pp. 158–9.)

As therefore, on the philosophical and religious side of his character, the cynic appears as a superior being, who looked down from an elevated station upon other men (being free from those relations in life by which other persons are confined), so also on the practical side he displays an excellence (which is yet very different from the Christian's meekness and love of enemies), viz., such an indifference to offences and inconveniences, that he cannot be affected by them. "The true cynic (he says) has no enemy, even when any one inflicts blows upon his body, or slanders and insults him; because enmity can exist only between persons who are on the same footing. But that virtue which is exalted above all strife can be honored only by love; and if any one be otherwise affected towards it (as many are even towards the gods), it is not felt as hostile or detrimental; but the rude person is looked upon as inflicting the heaviest punishment on himself, namely, an ignorance of his higher nature and a contented dereliction of its guidance." This cynicism, therefore, could be adapted only to some few extraordinary individuals; the multitude (he said) must follow the received opinions, as something better than entire shamelessness; for men in general have still some natural affinity with truth. The false cynics, on the contrary, he considered as men who impudently contemned received opinions without being justified therein by any superior talent or merit of their own; and who trampled under foot all the laws of society, though they introduced no better or purer mode of life, but one much worse and far more detestable.*

Christianity must have appeared to Julian, as he viewed it, a sort of false cynicism. He, indeed, compared that sort of cynics with the monks (called by him *ἀποτακτίσται*, men set apart). "For most of them (he says) have forsaken but very little property, and, in return for that little, they have scraped together what they could from all sides, and managed moreover to

* See Appendix XV.

get themselves great honor, a numerous retinue of servants and dependents. So it is with you, except that you do not make so much profit as they do; this however does not depend on you, but on us who have more sense than those silly people; and also because you have no pretext for collecting money in a reputable way, as they have, under the so-called name of alms. In every other respect you are like them; you have abandoned your father-land as they have; you go about in all directions; and ye are more burdensome to the court than they, and that with the more impudence, inasmuch as they are invited thither, whilst you are driven away."

According to Julian's view, every thing that is great and distinguished, in the inner as well as the outer life of man, in science and in art, is most intimately bound and connected with religion: and all this he derived from the influence of the gods and our communion with them. "As the mind of the gods (he says) is but seldom revealed, and only to a chosen few among men, not to all nor at all times, (all the oracles, for instance, had, after certain periods of time, lost their power,) so father Jupiter, the friend of man, unwilling that men should be altogether shut out from intercourse with the gods, imparts to them a knowledge of the sacred arts, that they may find in them the necessary helps for the uses of life." (Jul. *ap. Cyrill.* p. 189.) He considered therefore every extraordinary kind of strength or skill in art as an attribute of some god; he derived the origin of the same among men from the revelation of that god, to whom also he ascribed the care and provision for its due preservation. As the Greeks and Romans reverenced no god exclusively, but all with affection, so they also enjoyed the united gifts and imparted powers of those deities, and were admitted to the most correct notions respecting their nature. All the arts and sciences, whose imperfect germs commenced in barbarous nations, (as, for instance, astronomy among the Babylonians, geometry among the Egyptians, and arithmetic among the Phœnicians,) were, for the most part, applied by them only to the necessary uses of life, and remained each in an isolated, unconnected state. It was among the Greeks that they were first combined with each other, and received a higher intellectual direction.* (p. 173.)

"Apollo (he says, p. 155) has opened the oracles in all parts of the world, given divine wisdom to men, adorned cities with temples and political constitutions, communicated civilization and instruction by means of Greek colonies to the greatest part of the world, and so prepared them the more readily to submit to the Romans, who themselves were not only descended from the Grecian race, but also derived their religious practices and their religious faith entirely from the Greeks." "Therefore (he asserted, p. 252) they alone

* See APPENDIX XVI.

have treated philosophical subjects with success, have sought for truth by the right path of rational knowledge, and did not allow men, as most foreign nations do, to follow blindly the teaching of incredible legends." On account of this want of scientific cultivation (which operated upon them for the very reason that they did not reverence all the gods who had communicated those arts and powers to men, but one God exclusively) the Jews (he asserts) could form no perfectly pure idea of the divine nature, although they honored the true God in the right way. "The God of the Jews (he says) might perhaps have been a great God, and yet might have had† no good prophets and expositors; and the cause of this might be, that they had not previously purified their souls by scientific culture, and had not thereby opened the closed eyes of their understandings, nor extricated themselves from the surrounding darkness."† (*See Fragm. Ep, ad. Sacerd.*)

He believed that the religion of the Jews, inasmuch as it was a national religion, transmitted from holy progenitors, had something divine in its character, but that it had been gradually adulterated through the misunderstanding and ignorance of that people. "Although (he says, p. 354) I am one of those who are

* This single passage is enough to show that Julian, though *nominally* brought up as a Christian, was grossly ignorant of the Scriptures of the Old Testament, and therefore, probably, of the New also.—*T.*

† See APPENDIX XVII.

shy of joining with the Jews in celebrating their festivals, yet I always pray to the God of Abraham, of Isaac, and of Jacob, men who, being sprung from the holy, theosophic race of the Chaldæans, honored that God who, as a great and mighty Being, is gracious to me, and to all those who honor him as Abraham did." He also ascribed to the Jews oracles and myths which had a hidden meaning, the perversion of which he attributed to the fact, that these myths were understood by that rude people in their literal sense. "Moses certainly commanded the Israelites to honor only the one God who in a special manner presided over their nation, yet at the same time he names in connection with him other gods, and even forbids them to speak opprobriously of them (pp. 253 and 238) ; but the shameless insolence of the succeeding generations (who seemed to wish to banish all pious reverence from the hearts of men) advanced from not honoring to blaspheming the other gods. In all other respects, on the contrary, the Jews agreed with the practices of the Gentiles ; since they had temples, sacred groves,* sacrifices, and many religious usages which required the presence of the holiest sentiments."

But from the same cause which made Judaism an object of regard to Julian, Christianity must have ap-

* We have here another proof of Julian's ignorance, or perversion of Scripture facts ; for where is there any such prohibition of *speaking ill of false gods ?* and as for "sacred groves," are they not always associated with idolatry ?—*T.*

peared to him the more pernicious; since it was not merely the *corruption* of the Christian church that made that religion hateful to him before he made any distinction between the Christianity of his time and the form in which it *originally* appeared. [He had probably read the New Testament with attention, in his first search after truth, at the time when the doctrines of the church began to be suspected by him, and he thought he had discovered a falling off in the church of his time from the primitive teaching of Christianity.] Many ecclesiastical and symbolic forms, which the Christianity of that period (already departing more and more from its original simplicity) had adopted, must have harmonized much more with his view of religion, and might have helped rather to recommend Christianity to him; but its peculiar distinguishing character, its spirit, elevated above all forms, to the world that lies beyond this temporal existence, and especially the unpresuming lowliness that formed its very essence, were alike revolting to his imagination and his disposition. Christianity, as he viewed it, had nothing divine in its origin as Judaism had, but had its rise in a mixture of corrupted Judaism and heathenism; and therefore he applied to the Christians the name of Galileans, in order to show that they sprung from a race of men, despised even among the Jews, and composed of a mixture of Jews and heathens, *ἡ Γαλιλάια τῶν ἐθνῶν*, Galilee of the Gentiles. He saw in the

Christian religion a mixture of the egotistic rudeness of the Jews (which, transferring to the Deity the passions of men, spurned all other gods but the God of their nation) with that freedom from moral restraint* and contempt of holy practices, which was prevalent among the heathens. (*Ibid.* p. 238.)

When he says, "this religion claims to adapt itself to all nations, and to *men of all sorts, however different,* for instance, retail dealers, publicans, dancers," it is evident that he thought that a religion which pretended to such universal empire, with such adaptation to individual cases, must introduce confusion and disorder into society. For (he said) it would dissolve all the sacred and peculiar bands of individual states, as well as the ordinances instituted by the gods themselves, and made venerable by their high antiquity; nay, it must annihilate all love of country; and therefore he considered the fall of the Roman empire a consequence of the establishment of Christianity. "Through the folly of the Galileans (see his 7th Epistle) almost every thing has been ruined; but with the good-will of the gods we will support and maintain all once more." He was convinced that it was only through the works of the old Greek authors (written as

* I do not pretend, nor is it necessary, to notice Julian's fallacies or mistakes as they occur. If the German word "ungebundenheit," is here rightly rendered, it is obvious that he refers to "the liberty with which Christ has set us free," though he says nothing of the caution not to "use it as a cloak for maliciousness."—*T.*

they were under the direct inspiration of the gods) that elevated notions could be produced in men. According to his idea, every thing that is great and useful, of whatever kind, originated from a communion with the gods. Religion therefore could require no instruments of education foreign from itself, but would be self-sufficient to awaken and to cultivate all the powers and talents of men, scientific, political or warlike. In the holy Scriptures of the Christians, on the contrary, he could find nothing in reference to the peculiar institutions of political life, and none of those dazzling virtues which he sought to acquire. He therefore challenged the Christians to make the experiment of educating a child from its early days upwards, by means of these writings only, as he was sure that by the time that he had grown up into a man, he would be no better than a slave. (p. 230.)

As Christianity began its career with the dissolution of existing things, so (he asserted) it had in itself nothing fixed and enduring. It withdrew more and more from the institutions of its Founder, and mixed itself up with new inventions of men; Julian therefore asserted that neither St. Paul, nor any of the evangelists, presumed to speak of Christ as God. It was not till the multitude had begun to pay honors to the dead, that the evangelist St. John, and this in a concealed manner, introduced this doctrine. (Julian *apud. Cyrill.* l. x.) After which the Christians proceeded to still greater lengths in honoring the dead. On this point Julian believed that the Christians punished themselves; inasmuch as, being forsaken by the gods, they were subject to the dominion of the demons, who imparted to them that spirit of hatred and envy which was so foreign from the nature of the gods. Hence arose the fury with which they blasphemed the gods, threw down their altars, and persecuted one another on account of a difference in their opinions. Therefore it was that some of them retired to deserts in preference to cities, (though man was evidently made for society) being filled with a hatred of their kind by the suggestions of demons; nay, many of them even laid fetters* upon themselves.

In connection with Julian's peculiar views we must notice the plan which he adopted with regard to religious regulations in his dominions. He considered the prevailing coldness among the heathens, and their indifference towards the old religious institutions of their country, to be a cause of the spreading of Christianity; and he also looked upon the disreputable lives of the priests, and the contempt into which they had thereby fallen, as the result of their excessive riches, and their consequent love of pomp and luxury. His intention therefore was, in order to place the ancient religion once more on a firm foundation, to organize a new polythe-

* Julian probably refers to the bodily, self-inflicted castigations of the Anchorites. (See *Fragment. Epist. ad Sac.* 288.)

istic code of worship, which, as being dedicated to the gods, and out of regard to their spiritual operation, should be independent of the state, and before which all earthly rank and splendors should vanish ; in short, that it should, by the fact of its promoting sentiments of piety and philanthropy as well as religious information, refute the reproaches which the Christians cast upon heathenism. Julian here also himself set the strongest example. He not only took the title of Pontifex Maximus, as the other emperors had done ; but he prided himself in the priestly quite as much as in the imperial dignity, and discharged with equal conscientiousness the duties of supreme priest and emperor.*

As his occupations would not allow of his daily attendance at the temples remote from the palace, he erected within its precincts a temple to the god of the sun (Helios), as his especial patron and protector, and altars to all the gods ; since it was his fondest wish to live in constant communication with the gods, and to commence all his enterprises with their worship.† He sacrificed every day to the rising and the setting sun ; when engaged in the service of the gods he laid aside his imperial dignity, and wished not to be distinguished by any outward show before them. He might be seen himself running about and preparing all things for the sacrifice. He himself brought the wood together, and

* Libanius, 245. † Ibid., 282.

himself killed the victim (p. 246); and in thus acting, his object was to stimulate all the priests to the same degree of enthusiasm, and to fill them with the same conscientious desire to discharge the duties of their calling. This is attested by two of his epistles addressed to priests, which are remarkable records of his religious notions and of his plan for a renovated worship.* "Things are not yet (he writes to the high-priest of the Galatians) as I would have them in the Hellenic religion, and this is the fault of its professors. For that so great an alteration should have been wrought in so short a time is to be attributed to the *miraculous power of the gods;* yet we ought not to be contented therewith, but must try to counteract the causes through which *atheism* has so sadly gained the upper hand. These are, principally, the philanthropic treatment of strangers, the careful provision for the *burying of the dead,* and the respect gained by hypocritical pretences to a holy life. These virtues, whose false appearance† had been assumed by the Christians‡ in order to de-

* *Kirche* in the German; but I cannot render it "Church."—*T.*

† See APPENDIX XVIII.

‡ The heathens had early remarked in the Christians this active beneficence and brotherly love, this readiness to communicate to all their brethren from the remotest regions; and by a singular perversion, it induced them to look upon them with suspicion, as brothers of a secret order who recognized each other by mystic signs. (See Cæcil. *apud Minuc.*) To the cause second in order, Julian attached particular importance in the old religion, as through the neglect of the honors due to the dead he thought the manes, or infernal powers, were offended.

ceive, must all be practised in earnest by the Greeks; you must therefore oblige all the priests in Galatia to conform to a more respectable mode of life, or else depose them from their priestly office. They should never be seen in any theatre or any place of public resort; they should not engage in any unbecoming occupation; they should establish lodging-houses for strangers, and relieve with money not only Greeks but also strangers of other religious persuasions. In order to make this practicable to you, I have ordered thirty thousand measures of corn to be given yearly to the priests in all Galatia; one portion for the support of their servants, the rest for the relief of strangers and mendicants: since it would be shameful if, while among the Jews there are no beggars, and while the *Galileans* nourished not only their own but also heathen mendicants, the Greeks, on the contrary, do not even support their own poor. It is your duty to remind them themselves to contribute more to these means of relief, and to persuade the country people in their respective villages to dedicate their first-fruits to the gods.* I undertake to prove that this beneficent spirit is by no means peculiar to the Christian, but rather to the Grecian religion, having indeed been borrowed from the latter, to which it was peculiarly adapted. A saying of Homer's occurs to me, 'that all strangers and beggars are under the immediate pro-

* In imitation of the Christian oblations.

tection of Jupiter, under the titles of *Zeus xenios, homognios, hetairios.*' What a contradiction then is it to sacrifice to the god and at the same time to act contrary to his acknowledged character! It is not therefore to be laid to the charge of our religion, but of its professors, when they betray it by a conduct directly opposed to its spirit, and by so doing dishonor the gods."

The priests (he said) should take a lesson from the Christian bishops, and assert their dignity as superior to all earthly rank, claim respect from all officers of the state, and never humble themselves in their presence. If they have any business to transact with the governors of the province they should, in general, do it in writing, and rarely visit them in their houses; nor at their public entrance into the cities should any priest go out to meet them. No soldier should be allowed to attend the magistrates within the temple, since as soon as any one of them set foot upon the sacred threshold, he became a *private man;* the *priest* only possessed authority in the interior of the temple, as the law of the gods demanded. He exhorted the individual, whom he had made supreme priest in Asia, to observe strictly the old laws as they were given by the gods; for, he said, those laws had fallen into entire neglect through the prevailing love of riches and luxury, which in their turn had destroyed all piety; it was therefore necessary to take great care for an entire restoration of those laws *de novo.*

He begs (in his sixty-third Epistle) a philosopher of Cappadocia to point out to him there any one person who was truly devoted to the Hellenic religion; since he had hitherto seen many who were unfavorable to it, and only a few who, though certainly desirous of sacrificing, had yet no correct knowledge on the subject. (See also *Ep.* iv.) He has stated his ideas respecting the priesthood and its relation to the state, in the fragments of an Epistle to a priest, p. 288: "Certainly (he says) the civil power is bound by the laws of the state to take charge of the administration of justice; but the priests also ought to contribute towards it by their exhortations, that the sacred laws of the gods may not be transgressed." He defended, on the grounds already mentioned, the visible, sensible worship and adoration of images; yet so that not *merely* the *images* of the gods were to be worshipped, but also their temples, groves, and altars.

His idea also of the priestly character is a proof that the simple and original form of Christianity (which was directed only to the unseen, and disdained all merely human helps for its devotions) must have been much farther removed from Julian's view of religion than that form of it which was exhibited in his time. "The priests (said he) are to be honored as the servants of the gods, who as mediators between us and the gods, bring down good gifts to us from heaven; and since they sacrifice and pray for all, every one is bound to honor them even much more than the rulers of the state." He desired that the priests should be treated with universal respect, independent of their emoluments; "as long as any one is a priest, and is engaged in offering sacrifices for men and in attendance upon the gods, he must be treated with reverence and pious regard."

In his character therefore of *Pontifex Maximus*, he pronounced a kind of excommunication upon an official person who had insulted a priest. (See *Epist.* lxii.) "Even granting (he says) that an unworthy person exercised the priestly office, yet must he be treated with forbearance until his unfitness has been proved, and he has been excluded from the service of the temple. You know not, it would seem, the difference between a priest and a private person, as you have insulted one before whom you ought to rise up from your seat. Since therefore I am, by the usage of the country, the chief pontiff, I hereby exclude you from all religious service for the space of three months. If after that interval you shall appear worthy, and the chief priest of the city shall write to me to that effect, I will then again take counsel with the gods, and consider whether you shall once more be taken into favor."

"The priests (he says) must put away from them

every thing that is unsuitable to them in word and deed; the study of philosophy is most proper for them, especially the system of those philosophers who have taken the gods for their guides, who teach the existence and the providence of the gods, and that nothing evil can come from them. They should not appear at theatrical exhibitions, because of the improper pieces that are performed there. He was anxious to place them again in close connection with religion, and to bring them back to their original purity and dedication to Dionysos (Bacchus). During the time of the temple-service it becomes the priests to make use of splendid garments, but out of the temple only the ordinary plain dress; since it would be no trifling offence against the gods to use profanely the holy garments before the public, and allow them to be gazed upon by all men as something wonderful; as many impure persons might come in contact with them, and thus the sacred symbols of the gods would be desecrated.*

Julian sought to place the ancient religion in a new connection with the moral and intellectual education of the people, as well as to combine religious instruction with the public worship; an idea which he had borrowed from the Christian church, since public religious instruction was foreign from the polytheistic reli-

* Compare with this the Contest of Gregory the Great with John, bishop of Ravenna, about the use of the pallium except at the celebration of mass.

gion. He took also several other regulations from the Christian church, which in this respect appeared to him judicious; for instance, the Christian penitential ordinances, and the so called *epistolæ formatæ*, by which the remotest churches corresponded with each other; whereby a living sympathy was promoted among all the members of the church, and provision was made for the kind reception of strangers of whose character a sure testimonial was thus obtained. He instituted schools* in all the cities. After the example of the Christians, teachers of religion came forward in their public services, to explain, morally and philosophically, the sacred traditions and myths for the benefit of the hearers. The presidents (πρόεδροι) of these assemblies appeared adorned with purple and crowned with fillets.

"I have often remarked (says Gregory, when characterizing the polytheists of his time) that they affect what is venerable and extraordinary; as if that which is ordinary and of daily occurrence had somewhat contemptible in it, while the majestic had something in it which could at once infuse faith." Gregory places in contrast thereto the assemblies of the Christian, who looked for the high and exalted not so much in external appearance as in the moral character. "Their great effort (he says of the Christian teachers) is addressed to the inner man; they labor to lead their hearers to a thoughtful mind, and they have thereby

* See Gregor. *Orat. Stelit.* p. 69, ed. Montagu.

contributed very greatly to the improvement of the people." He thus accurately represents the consequences of the attempts which were being made to restore the ancient religion to life again by means of allegorical teaching: "In these allegories you propound your own fancies, but no one will be convinced by you; for a mere glance of the eye produces more conviction. So that you have not at all profited the hearer, while he who rests on that which meets his eye is offended."

Julian, in farther prosecution of his plan for placing the state in connection with religion, caused himself to be represented in the public statues, as receiving the crown and the purple from Jupiter appearing to him from heaven, whilst Mars and Mercury (since he affected at once the philosopher and the warrior) were looking on him with favoring eyes. (See Sozom. v. 17.) He was exhibited on his coins with a bull and an altar near him. (Socrat. iii. 17.) When his soldiers received a donative, an altar was erected on the place where the gift was distributed, and every one who wished to share in it was obliged to offer incense to the gods by way of thanks. (Gregor. *loc. cit.* 46.) The decay of religion and the decline of the arts and sciences were, in his estimate, most intimately related to each other; he sought therefore to elevate both at the same time. (Liban. *Orat.* x. p. 300.) He appointed, wherever he could, none but persons instructed in the ancient literature, to be his provincial lieutenants, and was greatly pleased when the cities sent delegates to meet him on his journeys who delivered well-written addresses to him. Consequently, the study of the literature which the emperor so highly favored, was every where pursued with fresh ardor. Many undoubtedly desired only to turn to their own advantage this inclination on the part of Julian, and imposed upon him by the assumption of the philosophic mantle.*

With a view of honoring the healing art, which "came down from heaven for the welfare of men, and as a relief for the weaknesses of our mortal nature," he declared all physicians, for the future, to be exempt from personal state-burthens. (See Julian's *Works*, p. 998.) With the view of promoting sacred music, he directed lads of good abilities at Alexandria, to be educated at the public expense, in order to become musicians; he promised still greater rewards to those of them who would study music in a scientific way; although (as he reminded them) they would themselves receive no trifling recompense in the mere fact, that their souls would be purified by the influence of sacred music. (p. 442.)

Julian showed himself in all respects a friend of ancient forms; since he considered them to be closely connected with the old religion and mental cultivation, the

* A fact which not only the partial Sozomen (iii. 1) relates, but also Libanius, Julian's admirer, gives us to understand, p. 308.

decay of which was, according to his view, a consequence of the barbarism attendant upon the decline of polytheism. And, because men no longer prayed to the gods alone as their lords and masters, they had become slaves to the caprice of an individual. On this account he particularly revived the old republican forms. He no longer, like the last emperors, summoned the senate to his palace, but took his place with the members of the senate, himself made public harangues, and allowed every one freedom of speech. (Liban. 298.)

As supreme ruler and chief pontiff of the Roman empire, he looked upon himself as bound to provide for the restoration and support of all national religions; for he thought they were all good in their way. He paid respect, therefore, even to Judaism (as we have noticed above), because it was a national religion; and, because he had heard from the Jews that they could sacrifice to their God in the right manner only in their temple at Jerusalem, he intended to have rebuilt it on a great scale of expense. (Sozom. iii. 20.) He relieved the Jews from the payment of taxes with which they had hitherto been oppressed, in order that they, being (as he wrote to them in his twenty-fifth Epistle) in the enjoyment of undisturbed repose on all sides, might pray the more earnestly for the success of his government, to the Almighty God, the Creator of all things, who had been pleased to crown him with his own pure hand. As men weighed down with cares naturally felt themselves also confined in spirit, unable to raise their hands with freedom in the act of prayer, he hoped they would thus be able to intercede for him with the mighty God, who could best direct his government to a successful issue; so that after the conclusion of the Persian war he might cause the holy city of Jerusalem (which he had wished for so many years to visit) to be again built up,* and unite with them within its walls to praise the Almighty.

* As Julian's chief object of aversion (like that of all apostates and seceders) was the religion which he had deserted, there was probably as much policy as piety in his patronage of the Jews, the bitterest enemies of Christianity.—*T.*

SECTION IV.

THE CONDITION OF THE CHRISTIAN CHURCH AT THE TIME OF THE EMPEROR JULIAN, AND THE TREATMENT IT RECEIVED AT HIS HANDS.

In order to form a better idea of Julian's conduct towards the Christian church, and its influence thereupon, we must consider the internal condition of that church, no less than its relation to the heathen. The alteration he aimed at in both these respects was the more strikingly felt, from the circumstance of the church having so lately been raised and favored by a power not its own, and having entered into a new relation therewith. Worldly advantages had become united with the reception of Christianity; advantages, which had induced many persons to go over to the Christian community, without any earnest efforts to attain to the true spirit of Christ's religion. In earlier times Christians had had an external contest to maintain, through which their faith was kept alive, and they themselves were made invincible against every assault. The contest the church had now to maintain was quite different and more arduous; *viz.* a contest with the world, which was no longer, as before, set in array against her, but sought on all sides to unite itself with her. It was through worldly desires that many persons, overpowering their appointed rulers, employed with insolence the preponderance which, by an adventitious strength, they had gained over their opponents. "The headstrong wickedness of the many (says Gregory, *loc. cit.*) gave Julian power against us; so also did the extreme prosperity of the Christians, with the corresponding changes which it must have introduced, the possession of power and honor, and the daring insolence naturally resulting therefrom." As soon as the Christian church has mixed itself up with that which is foreign to it, a corresponding re-action has, at all times arisen within itself, although the re-acting power has not always been clearly defined, and although the sect, which exhibited this reaction, has, in the course of its contest with the dominant church, gone to the other extreme, and thereby fallen into an error of another sort.

A re-action of this kind was produced at this time by the Donatists in Africa, although they proceeded with too little discretion, and too much excitement, to distinguish the simple truth, and to be able to remain firmly by it. The cry they raised amounted to this, "The church, through its connection with worldly interests, had degenerated from its original purity; it exercised a power that was contrary to the spirit of Christianity; it sought, contrary to the teaching of the Founder, a triumph by the help of worldly might, and to circumscribe that liberty of conscience which God has given to every man." An idea, therefore, arose among them, that amid the general corruption of Christians, the true church was preserved among *them* alone; an idea which occasioned that separation which must necessarily lead them still farther from the truth. A Donatist accordingly asserted, that Satan, who had hitherto conquered souls by the fear of torture, now, in times of peace, filled them with pride by flattering delusions, while he amused unhappy men with empty fame, and ensnared the avaricious with the friendship of princes and earthly presents.*

The Donatists therefore objected, at the religious conferences at Carthage, to the Catholic definition of the true church, *viz.*, "that it was the universal body of Christians dispersed through all the world." They maintained, in opposition to it, the schismatic definition, "that the Catholic name relates not to lands and nations, but to the completeness of the sacraments, and to the perfect, immaculate purity of the church." (p. 467, Du Pin.) This idea of the corruption of the church through its mixture with worldly associations, joined to the notion of Christian freedom which took possession of the minds of the common people, produced, by a strange misunderstanding, the wild extravagances of the Circumcellions.† [We may call to mind here the Peasant war‡ of Germany, and observe

* See Optat. *Miles de Schismate Donatist.* ed. Du Pin. p. 299.

† For a full account of the Circumcellions of Numidia, see Gibbon's *Rome*, iii. 398.—*T.*

‡ See Ranke's *Hist. of Reform.* Vol. ii. p, 203, for the Peasant war —*T.*

how similar causes have at different times produced similar effects.] Under the influence of such a persuasion they wished, without distinction, to place all ranks and conditions on the same footing; they seized upon the rich proprietors; they made the great men, whom they met upon the highways, descend from their carriages, put the slaves in their places, and compelled the masters to run before them as slaves (*loc. cit.* p. 56). The Donatists, moreover, were not displeased at the altered condition of the Christian church through Julian's succession to the Imperial government. It was quite right, according to their notions, that the temporal power was again separated from the church, and that things were thus brought back into their original state. They therefore presented an address to him, in which they spoke of him as the only ruler by whom justice was regarded.*

The Christian emperors (being deficient in a clear view of the relation of the church to the state and the proper limitations of both, and unable to conceive it right for any thing to be done in their dominions independently of their decision) had claimed to exercise the greatest influence upon ecclesiastical affairs. In consequence of this, the parties which understood how to take advantage of circumstances most adroitly, and could accommodate themselves best to the inclinations of those princes, got the upper hand. Such was the

* Augustin. *Eipst.* 166. Ed. Bas.

party of Ursacius, Valens, and Acacius; and these were naturally the most fluctuating in respect of theological opinions. On the contrary, those men who, like Athanasius, maintained a firm and consistent system, and defended it with firmness of character, without regard to time and circumstances, were subjected to extreme opposition. Julian, however,* recalled the exiled ecclesiastics, and gave all parties among the Christians equal liberty, with the hope that by their mutual contentions they would destroy one another, and not be able to unite for the purpose of a common defence. It now appeared (as the consequence of the removal of external pressure) that the artful practices through which many Christian teachers had labored for the predominance of their party, were all in vain, and that the final victory of one side or the other must now depend on their own strength.

With respect to the relation in which the Christians then stood towards the heathen, we must recollect that, before the *sole* reign† of Constantius, the two parties engaged in a contest with each other, and that their relative position was very different in different provinces. After an actual religious war (for such it was, although the external occasion of the war between the princes was quite of another kind) the Christian party had gained the upper hand; and the

* Socrat. iii. 1.

† *i. e.* his coming to the entire power, which he had at first shared with his brothers.—*T.*

result was such as usually attends upon victory in a religious war. The victorious party occasionally behaved with arrogance to the conquered; and, under the government of the Christian emperors, sometimes tumultuous bodies of Christians, sometimes individual bishops, tore down splendid temples and altars in many places. Of course the displeasure of the heathens at seeing their holy places destroyed before their eyes must have risen the higher, because they were forced to conceal it, and highest of all in places where, as the greater number, they felt conscious of their preponderance, and yet dared not make use of it. With this tone of feeling it required no imperial edict to excite a persecution. Let but the external pressure cease to act, let the emperor allow a glance of favor towards the old religion to escape him, the offended parties rushed unbidden to wreak a furious vengeance for their long-endured oppression.* We must always keep in view this relation of the two parties to each other, if we would judge fairly of *Julian's conduct towards Christianity and the Christian church.*

Gregory Nazianzen justly observes, that an empe-

* Similar scenes were exhibited even under the later emperors. In the reign of Honorius, *e. g.*, soon after he had solemnly forbidden the public exercise of heathen worship, a savage insurrection of the heathens against the Christians broke out in the Numidian city of Calame, where the latter formed the minority. The immediate cause was a festive procession, which the heathen population conducted in front of the church doors of the Christians. (See Augustin. *Epist.* 202. Ed. Bas.)

ror who would have ventured to attack the Christian church at that period, must have excited an apprehension of a civil war; and also, that many of the consequences, usually attendant upon internal religious divisions, had actually exhibited themselves already. "To wish (he says)* to shake the Christian church, is nothing else than to throw into disturbance the whole Roman empire, and to stir up danger for the entire state, discord between nations and cities, separation of families and houses; all this must follow in the train of that master-evil; in fact, it has already followed therefrom." This struggle could not but break out first and most violently in Asia Minor, where through the flourishing study of ancient literature and the Platonic philosophy in Ionia, the old religion was most warmly supported, where the splendid temples operated most strongly on the minds of the people, and where the destruction of some of them had most violently excited the general indignation. The same might be said of Alexandria, where the population were in the most unsettled state, and most easily led to any violent expression of fanaticism. Under the last emperor the heathens in this city had experienced the greatest oppression from the cruel Arian bishop, George, who by acting the part of a *delator*, or public accuser, and for having caused many temples to be thrown down, had made himself an object of general hatred. At last, as

* *Orat. Stelit.* p. 41.

he was passing one day by an ancient temple of *Τύχη*, the Goddess of Fortune, he said in the hearing of the Pagans, "How much longer shall this *tomb* stand here?" The Christians, before the eyes of the Pagans, derided the mysteries of Mithra, the god of the Sun, having caused a church to be built in the place where these mysteries were wont to be celebrated. All this provoked the rage of the heathens, which broke out with the more violence because they had so long been obliged to repress it. The results were scenes of bloodshed in the city and sad divisions in families. George was the victim of these embittered feelings, though the Christians might have saved him, had he not made himself an object of hatred to the greater part of the Alexandrian Christians by his persecution of the Athanasian party.*

The popular fury was in a great measure occasioned by cruel and inhuman executions of individual Christians (if we may here venture to trust the accounts of the Christian historians) in the cities of the Lesser Asia, and especially of Phrygia, where the Pagan party appears to have been by far the majority.† These savage persecutions fell generally upon individuals only, as upon Marcus, bishop of Arethusa, who had endeavored, in the preceding reign, to bring the Hellenistic inhabitants to adopt Christianity, not by

* Ammian. 15. 11. Socrat. iii. 2.

† See Sozom. v. 9—11. Greg. Naz. *loc. cit.* pp. 50—54.

dint of instruction,* but by compulsory measures. We may instance also the case of some Christians in the Phrygian city of Mero, who had dashed to pieces the images which had shortly before been re-erected in a temple; as well as that of Basilius, a presbyter of Ancyra, who, not satisfied with exhorting the Christians of the neighborhood to be true to the faith, drew upon himself the anger of the people by interrupting a heathen sacrifice. We must connect with this the fact, that Julian every where attached great consideration to the persons of the priests; that they undoubtedly excited the people to frequent violence against the Christians; and, that wherever he could, he appointed as governors those persons who were zealously devoted to the old religion, or at least affected to be so, in order to please the emperor.

That no general persecutions arose from these tumultuous executions, that a contest between the parties was not produced by the support which the Christians gave to their zealous teachers, seems to prove that in these cities the Pagans constituted by far the majority of the population, and that only a few persons were to be found there who had gone over to Christianity from a free disinterested attachment. Those few examples of a bloody persecution of the

* Προθυμότερον ἢ κατὰ πείθω, says Sozom. Gregory is not so impartial, who says that he made use of no other means than the excellence of his life and the force of his eloquence.

Christians could therefore, under these circumstances, afford no well-grounded cause of accusation against Julian. Indeed, persecutions and compulsory conversions were by their very nature contrary to his principles; and not only to his principles of policy, as the Christian historians assert, (forasmuch as he had seen in former persecutions how greatly the death of martyrs contributed to the spreading of their religion,) but also to his religious and philosophical principles. His notion of the gods was that they could not properly be said to *take offence* at any thing, as if they were revengeful beings, delighting in punishment; since envy and hatred were unknown to them, and proper only for demons.

He thus writes to a priest: "Those Christians only ought at once to be punished who are rebellious against the emperor; since in not serving the gods they have already punished themselves; and having relinquished the protection of the gods, they are driven on by wicked demons."* He considered it an affront to the gods, "when Christians, who had been dedicated by baptism to the service of demons, visited the temples with impure minds, and were forced to sacrifice to the gods against their will. They ought beforehand (as he himself had done on his assumption of the government) to release themselves by an expiatory offering† from the pollution of baptism." Yet he wrote thus from

* Fragment. *Ep. ad Sacerdot.* † 'Αποτροπαῖον.

Antioch (in August A. D. 362) to the citizens of Bostra: "He exhorted as well the Pagan as the Christian inhabitants not to annoy or disturb one another; that men should be operated upon not by violence, but by instruction and argument; the unhappy deserved compassion rather than hatred; the highest good consisted in the true reverence of the Deity; the greatest evil was a godless mind; it was by that very godlessness that those persons were mostly punished, who turned away from the gods to pay honors to the *dead* and to their *remains*." (p. 437. Compare *Ep.* xliii.)

To this was added, that Julian was very reluctant to give occasion, in any way, for the suspicion that his religious impressions arose more from a superstitious fear of the gods, than from a pious and thoughtful mind.* It may also be asked, "whether (with his views of religion, and state, and science in their mutual relation, and agreeably to his plan of placing religious and political regulations in the same close connection in which they were associated of old) he was not obliged to rob the Christians of many civil advantages, which he considered to have been inseparably attached to the original national religion?" It was natural that Julian, who no longer acknowledged the Christian as the dominant church, should deprive it of all those privileges which the Christian emperors had conceded to

* Ὑπὸ δεισιδαιμονίας μᾶλλον ἢ διανοίας εὐσέβους καὶ λελογισμένης. *Orat.* 7. p. 204.

it; and certainly most of them had been occasionally abused. Accordingly, he took away from the churches the allowance of corn which had been assigned to them;* from the clergy, immunity from state-burthens,† and exemption from attendance in the courts of law; indeed the bad consequences of those privileges might well induce him to do this, since many persons, to the injury of the state, and from merely external considerations, had sought exemptions from these duties by assuming the clerical character.‡ He also took from them the jurisdiction which to a certain extent had been conceded to them, as well as the right of making wills and receiving legacies; a privilege which, before the time of Constantine, had been interdicted to the clergy, as a *secret association.*§ He might have had good reason for reproaching them with having abused these privileges in order to assume dominion, to appropriate the goods of others, and bring every thing into their own power. Indeed later church-writers‖ complained thereof, and expressed their disapprobation and regret, not so much at the act of Valentinian in curtailing these rights of the clergy, as at the fact of their having deserved it.

The effect of Julian's wish to place the affairs of

* See Sozom. v. 15. † Liturgiis.

‡ Julian, *Ep.* ii. p. 380. § Ἑταίρεια.

‖ Ambrose, *Ep.* 52. Hieronym. *Ep.* 51. *de vita et moribus clericorum,* (quoted in Gibbon, IV. 273.)—*T.*

state once more in the closest connection with religion, would at once be to bring the Christians into many critical collisions. He caused himself (as has been already mentioned) to be represented in his images in strict association with the gods, not perhaps at first to irritate the Christians (as Gregory accuses him of doing), but to show his gratitude to the gods, and, perhaps also, with the view of accustoming men, by familiarizing their eyes to such sights, to consider the state and the national religion as things most closely interwoven with each other. When now the Christians took offence at this, and refused, because of it, to pay the customary mark of respect* to the images of the emperor, the magistrates, with a show of justice, though in fact with great injustice, might easily consider them disobedient to the laws of the state in thus refusing due honor to its head. His object (according to Gregory, *loc. cit.* p. 45) actually succeeded with the multitude, who, without being aware of it, paid homage at once to the image and to the gods. Some, however, who refused to comply, were punished as offenders against the imperial majesty ; nevertheless, this is not sufficient ground for an accusation against Julian himself, since Gregory does not accurately state the attending circumstances, nor make it clear whether such punishment ought not to be laid to the charge of particular governors.

* *προσκύνησις*.

The facts of the case,* probably, refer (like many others) to the soldiers only. The emperor, it is clear, had an especial interest in causing them to pay homage to the gods, since he was convinced that success in war could come only from the gods, that they alone could give courage and strength, and that the Christian religion, on the contrary, made men effeminate and powerless. It is undoubted, even according to the confession of Libanius, that he committed the highest offices to pagans, from whom alone he expected fidelity, and by whose help only he could hope to attain his great object, the union of the state with the public religion. According to the Christian historians† (though the charge is perhaps expressed by them in too general terms) he every where excluded the Christians from all appointments of authority, whether as judges or magistrates. Socrates, indeed, quotes as Julian's assigned motive, that it was because the doctrines of their religion forbade them to use the sword against those who had deserved capital punishment. This, however, might only have been irony and ridicule, after Julian's accustomed manner, to indicate, how little of earnestness there was in the professed principles of the Christians, how greatly they thereby deceived men, and how widely their lives were at variance with those principles, and how little their doctrines, when taken in their strictness, were applicable to social life.

* According to Sozom. v. 17. † Sozom. v. 18. Socrat. iii. 13.

It may, however, have been seriously intended by Julian; he had perhaps heard that Christian governors had entertained religious scruples against the infliction of capital punishment, and had asked advice* thereon from Christian teachers; that these teachers had, by their intercession, released many criminals from the punishment assigned to them by the laws; and he therefore believed that the order of things as fixed by the laws was in danger of being disturbed.† Another edict, by which the Christians were forbidden to institute public schools of rhetoric and literature, is liable to be unfairly judged of, unless we at the same time take into our consideration Julian's view of religion and science. He was convinced that the great writers of antiquity had produced all their works solely by the aid of the gods, to whom every art is dedicated; that therefore a belief in these gods, and proper notions respecting them, were not merely by accident, but ne-

* Thus Studius, an officer of the empire, submitted his doubts on the subject to Ambrose, bishop of Milan. (See Ambrose's *Epist.* 25.) It is certain, however, that these intercessions of the bishops (though in particular cases they might have been injurious through the abuse of social order, owing to the caprice of a despotic government, the defective constitution of the provinces, the rank of the parties at court, and the commotions thereby excited) were on the whole exercised for very salutary purposes. (See Augustine's *Ep.* 225, and many other vouchers in his Epistles.) Christianity, breathing as it does a spirit of mercy and kindness, first generally introduced into the administration of justice a more moral aspect, and a milder procedure corresponding therewith, according to the different circumstances of the different nations which were subject to her instruction.

† See Augustin, *Epist.* 53.

cessarily connected therewith, so that the one could not have arisen without the help of the other.

"The gods" (he says in his edict),—"the gods were taken as the guides of their respective talents by Homer, Herodotus, and Thucydides; one attached himself to Mercury, another to the sacred Muses. It seems incorrect, therefore, that those who despised the gods whom these great men honored, should act as expositors of their works. If they esteemed for their wisdom the writings which they undertook to explain, they should first desire to imitate the pious reverence of the writers of whom they would be the expositors. But if they think that they have erred in the weightiest matters, they had better confine themselves to the task of expounding Matthew and Luke in the churches of the Galileans." He asserted in another place, that a person who had been brought up solely in the study of such writings must prove himself unfit for every thing else, and incapable of every exalted sentiment in actual life. It appeared therefore to him unjust in the extreme, that Christianity, which despised the gods, and yet could not support itself by its own strength, should make use of their gifts in order to appropriate to itself that in which it was deficient.

Already, in the third century, Porphyry makes it a matter of accusation against Origen, that he made use of the philosophy of the Greeks in order to give a better appearance to his religious teaching; that he introduced Platonic notions into the same by means of allegorical interpretation;* and Julian, during the early part of his education in Cappadocia, had had especial opportunities of becoming acquainted with the school of Origen, which was then predominant. He looked upon those writings partly as religious documents, and believed therefore that he ought not to allow them to be made despicable to the youth of his country, by means of public teachers who borrowed from them just what pleased them, that is, only their external form. "All teachers of youth (he said), and especially the Sophists, who profess to be not only teachers of the outward expression, but also of moral and political philosophy, ought to be men of honest intentions, who would not bring with them opinions at variance with the established religion. But those Christian teachers, by means of the praise they bestowed upon the ancient classics, allured the young men to them, and in this manner deceived them, whilst they implanted their own wrong notions in their minds."

Let this edict of a polytheist Emperor, who wished to re-establish the old constitution of the state, be compared with the judgment of a cotemporary Christian teacher, Tertullian (for the regulations were still in force), who forbade the Christians to *institute* schools of literature, because they could not avoid being mixed up with the religious regulations of the state, and be-

* See Euseb. *Hist. Eccl.* vi. 19.

cause they would be obliged to learn the genealogies of the gods and take part in the celebration of their festivals.* The same authority however held it to be allowable, nay even necessary, to *attend* the schools of literature, because without the profane sciences the sacred ones could not be properly learnt. Just so Julian also, though on opposite principles, permitted all young men who wished it to attend those schools. Gregory indeed finds bitter fault with Julian for having grudged to the Christians that which is the common right of all rational beings, as if it were the peculiar privilege of the Hellenists. And so it must have appeared to the Christians, though not necessarily so to Julian, who looked upon this Classical learning as the property of a particular god and of the nation devoted to his worship.

Julian nevertheless was disposed, upon quite different grounds, to permit the Christians, like every body else, to enjoy without interruption all the other advantages of civil society; since he considered it a point of honor to re-establish in the state the former order of legitimate government, and to banish that arbitrary rule which had prevailed under the last emperors. He therefore expressed his displeasure at the insurrection of the people of Alexandria in which George had been murdered; and this he did, though he approved of

* For instance, the Quinquatria, Minervalia, &c. Tertullian, *de Idololatria*, p. 733.

their cause,* and ascribed it to his special regard for them that he did not punish them severely. We do not find however any instance of his actually punishing the townspeople who had ill-treated the Christians; for the Emperor was always pleased at a display of enthusiasm in the cause of the gods and of zeal against their enemies. He believed also that they had deserved such treatment by their previous acts of violence; his exhortations, therefore, could by themselves have but little effect.

We must make an especial distinction between Julian's conduct to the Christians in general and his behavior to the bishops. He believed that "the former, who had hitherto erred only from ignorance of the truth and from being deceived by their teachers, would easily allow themselves to be led back again to the religion of their fathers" He therefore sought to corrupt them with bribes, and to accustom them by degrees to the worship of the gods; indeed he seems to have hoped that, "as the Christian doctrines were not firmly imprinted in their minds, they would gradually be cured of their error by the divine power associated with that service." But he could have no such hope in regard to the bishops, "who were so confirmed in their erroneous views and so zealous in defending them." It was not therefore his design (as he himself says) to allow the banished bishops to recover the pos-

* *Epist.* 10.

session of their offices in the church, but only to return home to their country. In his first edict against Athanasius, who still defended the Christian doctrines with undaunted and unwearied zeal, he at first only expressed his displeasure that, having been banished by the command of the late emperor, he had, in his insolence and without waiting for the imperial permission, immediately resumed his bishoprick, to the great vexation of the Alexandrians. He accordingly banished him from the city. (See *Epist.* 26.)

In his second edict (*Ep.* 6) he expressed very plainly the reason of his displeasure ; viz., that Athanasius was spreading a contempt for all the gods, and had carried his audacity so far as to persuade respectable females of the Hellenistic religion to submit to baptism. By his last edict (*Epist.* 51) he banished him entirely from Egypt, and wrote afterwards to the people of Alexandria, that if they wished still to continue in the error of the Galileans, they should at least be agreed among themselves ; and as to Athanasius, they need not long for, or regret him, since they could find many persons among his scholars equal to him in religious knowledge, who could take the direction of their spiritual instruction as well as he. But if they longed after him on account of his *cleverness* and *sagacity* in other respects, he would have them know that he was banished on that very account ; as it would be hazardous to leave a restless man, who thought it a great thing to put his life in danger, at the head of such a population. This indeed was generally a sufficient reason with Julian for thinking that he ought to be severe with the bishops, because he made it so great an object to enforce the legitimate order of things; and he looked upon them as disturbers of the public peace, who paid no regard to human authority.

In this spirit he wrote to the citizens of Bostra: "The clergy, because they can no longer exercise their former power and dominion, endeavor to put the people in commotion and cause an insurrection, in contempt of my imperial commands; I exhort therefore all the citizens to take no part in the tumultuary proceedings of the clergy, nor allow themselves to be urged on by them to throw stones, or to any other act of disobedience to the authorities. You may however assemble together as much as you please, and join in such prayer as ye may think good." The clergy of this city had justified themselves before the emperor on this charge of insurrection, by explaining to him, that the Christians, though equal in number to the polytheist inhabitants, were kept quiet by their means. Julian made use of it in order to make them objects of suspicion with the laity as their accusers, and called upon the citizens to expel them as such from the city. He might indeed occasionally have had his bad opinion of the bishops confirmed by their conduct, as when Mavis, bishop of Chalcedon, publicly denounced him in Constantinople as a godless man; and he punished him at the time for the offence.*

In all these cases we ought to remember Julian's peculiar character, as it expressed itself in the other particulars of his conduct. Undoubtedly he had undertaken the task of re-establishing justice and legitimate order in the administration of government, after they had been so capriciously destroyed in the preceding reigns. It was his wish to extend the enjoyment of equal rights to all his subjects; but his ardent nature could easily, on particular occasions, be inflamed to violent passion and unjust partiality, which hurried him into actions unsuitable to his character.† He was however conscious of his failing; he was sorry for such behavior, and exhorted his prefects and his friends to call his attention to the fact, whenever he suffered himself to be carried away by passion or party feeling.‡ In general therefore he remained true to his principles of religious toleration, and could act agreeably to them (as far as they consisted with his religious opinions), and yet at particular moments he could be led away by his impetuosity to act contrary to those principles. A contradiction might accordingly display itself in his conduct, which gave occasion for the charge brought against him by Gregory Nazianzen, "that these principles were but empty declamation;" —which certainly was not the case.

* Sozom. v. 4. † Ammian. 22. 3. ‡ Ammian. 22, 1.

Thus we read that the emperor (when he took upon himself the duty of administering justice at Antioch, and even pronounced sentence on the disputed matters) could not resist the temptation of asking the contending parties, "What religion they professed?"* Yet his justice showed itself the more remarkably, since, according to the narrative of the same historian we have referred to, it does not appear that he ever decided in a single case contrary to what was just; though on the part of the Christian who lost his cause, his *question* might well give occasion for the suspicion, that Julian had acted unjustly towards him on account of his religion. To this may be added the ironical, jeering answers which he occasionally made to the complaints of the Christians. For instance, when he ordered the church property of the Arian Christians (who, contrary to all established order, had committed acts of violence against the Valentinians) to be taken from them, "in order (as he rudely said) that they might make the path to heaven easier, according to the precept of their admirable Founder." Or when in reply to some Christians, who complained to him of unjust treatment, he answered, "that they ought, according to the instructions of the Gospel, to submit with patience to every offence." As to his threats, he seems to have sought to alarm rather in sport than in earnest; reports nevertheless might well arise, that he intended

* Marcellin. *ibid.*

to prevent the Christians from all public assembling together, from the exercise of all civil rights, and generally from all the advantages of political associations.*

It belonged to Julian's character (agreeably to the motto of his family, "*a proposito nusquam declinare*,"†) never to permit himself to be driven from his plans by any obstacle in the execution of them, but rather to persevere in them so much the more zealously; and especially in a plan which had sprung from the very inmost recesses of his mind. Had he lived a longer life, he would probably (whilst following up his favorite idea, and embittered by the opposing spirit of the times) have excited the most violent commotions, till perhaps he would himself have fallen a sacrifice to his own idolized conception.

The conduct of Julian during his residence in Antioch (in the year of our Lord 362, before he set out upon his expedition against the Persians) gives a good idea of the man himself, in altered times, and with men of different minds, pursuing the idea of olden times, that was ever floating before him. He affected to appear in the simple greatness of ancient heroes, himself administering justice, and, in the very centre of oriental luxury and splendor, occupied solely with the cares and concerns of government. He would have

* Sozom. v. 18. Gregor. *loc. cit.* p. 57.
† Ammian. 22, 14.

men serve only the gods and the laws, and the latter only as being hallowed by the former.* He utterly declined the barbarian title of δεσπότης, maintaining that all persons should appear on a par before the gods. He himself assisted, as a servant of the priests, in bringing in the victims;† and unattended, during violent rain, in the open air, sacrificed to the presiding gods in order to avert from the city the evils of an unproductive season.‡ When he saw many of the most distinguished inhabitants pouring into the temple, not so much for the purpose of worshipping the gods as to flatter the emperor, (whom they received with loud acclamation as in a theatre,)§ he made them feel his displeasure at their adulation offered not to the gods but to man, reminding them that even the gods should not be addressed with flattery, but with the reverent worship of a calm mind.

By the complete contrast of his manners and principles with the tone of mind of those with whom he was residing, he drew upon himself the ridicule and hatred of the higher classes, who took no great interest in the matter of religion, and became odious to the common people as an enemy to Christianity: so that both parties longed again for the rule of Christianity and Constantius, or, as they briefly expressed it in

* See Julian's *Misopogon,* p. 343.

† Ammian. 22, 14. ‡ Liban. *Legat. Julian.* 163.

§ *Misop.* 344. Liban. 41.

Greek characters,* for X and for K. He had undertaken to restore in all their splendor the oracle and the worship of Apollo, which had been celebrated of old in the grove of Daphne,† near Antioch. He caused, therefore, the temple to be surrounded with a magnificent peristyle, and the bones of the martyr Babylas (over which the Cæsar Gallus had built an oratory, in order to turn away the *religio loci* from Apollo to Christ) to be exhumed. No sooner was this done, than men and women, young children and gray-headed Christians, bore away the coffin in solemn procession to another place, singing as they went the Psalms which refer to the destruction of idolatry.‡

He hoped to see the festival of the Daphnian Apollo, the national feast of the Antiochians, again celebrated with the greatest splendor after its long discontinuance. Let us hear his own words which best express the disappointment of his expectation: "I hastened from the temple of Jupiter to the sacred grove, in the hope that I should there be gratified with the greatest display of your riches and your love of show. I already pictured to myself the festive processions,

* In his *Misopogon*, Julian complains that the people (of Antioch) returned him evil for good, and calumniated him for the good name he had acquired; that they accused him of having turned all things topsy-turvy: *ὅτι παρ' ἐμοῦ τα τοῦ κοσμοῦ πράγματα ἀνατέτραπται, καὶ ὅτι πολεμῶ τῷ Χῖ· πόθος δὲ ὑμᾶς εἰσεῖσι τοῦ Κάππα.*—*T.*

† See Gibbon, iv. 118.—*T.*

‡ See Sozom. v. 29.

and saw by anticipation the victims and the holy choirs, the rows of youths attuning their voices in honor of the god, and dressed in garments of dazzling whiteness. But when I entered the grove I saw no burning of incense, no wafer-cakes, no victims! I was at first amazed, though I endeavored to believe they were only on the outer skirts of the grove, waiting, out of compliment to me as the Pontifex Maximus, for a signal from me for their entrance. When, however, I inquired of the priest, 'What offering does the city intend to bring to-day in honor of the annual festival of the god?' he answered me, 'I bring from my own house a goose, as an offering to Apollo; but the city has prepared nothing for him!'"

The emperor, whom this scene must have sorely annoyed, reprimanded the Senate in a set speech: "Every one of you (he said) allows his wife to give all she has to the Galileans; you support the poor amongst them by your goods, and thereby promote greatly the spread of atheism among the people. You give large and splendid entertainments on *your own* birthdays, and yet no one brings even a little oil for the lamps at the festival now, after so long an interval, revived, nor the smallest offering for the god." As the emperor entered the temple in this state of feeling, he fancied that the god, through the medium of his image, gave him indications, that, being offended at the absence of religious feeling in the people of Antioch, he would no longer fill their temple with his presence. Soon after the fire broke out which consumed the temple and the image of the god. All these circumstances taken together so greatly exasperated Julian against the Christians, that, without any ground of evidence, he considered them as the authors of the conflagration. He caused the principal church at Antioch to be shut up; he ordered the Christian chapel, which had been built near the temple of Didymean Apollo, near Miletus, to be thrown down; and acted towards the Christians of Antioch with more severity than he had ever been accustomed to do.

Julian continued consistent with himself to the last. Regardless of his own safety, in a contest for a notion which had taken possession of him (*viz.*, the subjugation of the barbarians, the Persians), he found in battle (A. D. 363) a brilliant heroic death, suitable to those ideas of former times that were ever present to his soul. His faith in the divine origin and destiny of man, (a faith which may itself be divine, though the dogmas by which it is materialized are of men,) and his belief in the wisdom of remote antiquity, inspired him with an enthusiasm which raised him above the things of time, and did not leave him to his last moment. As he rushed into the thick of the fight, unmindful of the danger to which he exposed himself, he received a mortal wound from a hostile javelin. As soon as his wound had been bound up and the violence of the pain somewhat relieved, he hastened back to the support of his troops; but the powers of his body could not keep pace with his will. Having been carried back to his tent, his first care was to console his friends; he exhorted them not to lament for their commander, who was going to heaven and to the stars. He then, as long as he could breathe with sufficient ease, conversed with the philosophers Maximus and Priscus (who always accompanied him) on the exalted nature of the soul. When respiration at length became difficult, he took a draught of cold water, and expired—at the early age of thirty-two.*

* See Ammian. Marcell. xxv. 3.

APPENDIX.

APPENDIX.

No. I. (p. 19.)

PHILOSOPHY began and ended its first career with skepticism; but the skepticism with which it began was very different from that with which it ended. Religious ideas were at first propagated among men by tradition, independent of all speculation, which does not appear to have come in contact with them, at their first awakening. As in the natural course of things, man is every where led by that which lies most remote to that which is nearest and most interesting to him; as he is awakened to a consciousness of himself by the contrast of an external world which he cannot penetrate, (although this internal consciousness, according to the course of nature, precedes the external one,) so his first attempt at speculation was produced by the opposition existing between the *unity* of the human mind and the *plurality* of the world external to it.

"Because they were astonished," says Aristotle in his *Metaphysics*, i. 2, "men first began to philosophize; and their wonder was at first excited by that only which was less difficult of comprehension, that, for instance, which lay before their eyes; they then advanced gradually farther and farther, and proposed questions concerning greater things, such as the sun, moon, and stars, and so at last concerning the origin of the universe. Then began the attempt to comprehend generally how the variety of appearances which they saw around them, can be combined with the unity that reveals itself in this ever-recurring state of change; and how the scene on which this alteration takes place remains still the same, while every thing therein is subject to change in ever-varying forms, but still according to fixed and uniform laws." The first philosophers, therefore, believed that matter* was the cause of all changes, since they observed that every thing proceeded from it and again returned to it. This, that was thus the foundation of all existences, seemed itself ever to exist the same, only presenting itself in different forms and appearances. They looked therefore upon this matter as the element of all, and upon all other things and appearances only as metamorphoses and different affections thereof; while, in fact, nothing *really* originated, or ceased to be.† This was the first, or materalizing *Pantheism.*

The human understanding, advancing farther, found that even this fundamental unity was only an arbitrary abstraction, a creation of the human mind, and that no such unity existed any where; but, on the contrary, that every thing which appeared to be *one* was at the same instant also a *plurality;* that in short nothing *exists*, but that there is every where a perpetual movement only and progressive growth; that neither in nor out of man is there any thing fixed or durable, but every where and always a mere state of fluctuation. This was the first dogmatic *skepticism*, which looked upon non-existence as the only certainty; and from this system, so destructive of all natural sentiment, arose the Sophistic School of the time of Socrates. Both parties, as well the pantheistic materialist as these skeptic philosophers, tended necessarily to the destruction of piety and morality. To this was added (since the phenomena of the political world are wont to be in strict connection with those of the moral and intellectual world) that capricious arrogance, which through the unbridled democracy of Athens, and the civil wars of the Greeks, despised the restraints of law, and disregarded divine and human rights alike.‡

At this time, and in opposition to this mode of thinking, arose *the true philosophy* which reduced man's arrogant understanding to its proper limits, brought man back again *to himself* and to the consciousness of that which is nearest and most deeply seated in him, as well as of that which is highest *above* him, independent of and exalted beyond all power of reflection. At the same time it carried in itself the proof of its certainty, while it united with this inner conviction a corresponding confirmation of the traditions and ordinances of the ancient religion. Such was the spirit and object of the *So-*

* Principium ex quo. † *Metaphys.* i. 3. † See Thucyd. iii. 82.

cratic philosophy. Plato expressly mentions two parties, one of whom taught that nothing was *real* but what could be grasped with the hands, that even *acting* and *being* were nothing; the other maintained, that all was but *motion* (that which put, or was put in motion, being nothing), and that we must wholly strike out from our language all expressions that implied any fixity or real existence.* The *later* skepticism was very different from the arrogance of the *earlier;* being the skepticism of the understanding directed against its own dogmatism, and brought to a consciousness of its utter groundlessness and uncertainty.

No. II. (p. 25.)

This resembles the argument on which Romanism always rests its pretensions; viz., that the man who does not secure for himself a firm basis for his faith as it is offered to him by the authority of the Church, must for ever be doubting and seeking, and yet can never arrive at any thing like certainty. "Si quia alia tanta ab aliis sunt instituta, propterea in tantum quærere debemus, in quantum possumus invenire, *semper quæremus* et *nunquam* omnino *credemus.* Ubi enim erit finis quærendi?" (See Tertullian, *Præscript. adv. Hæretic.*) Bossuet also appealed to the same argument (in his *Reflexions sur un écrit de M. Claude*), "that according to the teaching of Protestants there is a time in the life of every Christian when he must necessarily be in doubt whether the Holy Scriptures be from God, or not; while, on the contrary, in him who is born in the lap of the Church, faith in her, and in all that is handed down through her, precedes all inquiry." In this manner the authority of a standing Church has always flattered the efforts and longing after repose in the individual who dreads a struggle with himself and shrinks from a state of doubt. But does it not seem agreeable to the general analogy of actual life, that men should arrive at repose only through a previous contest? and that the *great event* which presented itself as the *Redemption* in the history of man (its common centre and point of unity) should still anew make itself known to men as their means of safety and release from this αἰων πονηρός, this wicked world?

* *Thæetet.* Bip. Edit. Vol. ii. p. 76, *et seq.*

No. III. (p. 44.)

ORIGEN answered Celsus by a striking allegory, taken from the narrative of the building of the Tower of Babylon: "In the beginning all men spoke one language, the language of truth; but through their departure from heavenly pursuits they lost this, and therefore a variety of different languages was introduced. And so it went on, till Christianity brought back that universal language, and released men from the peculiar laws to which particular nations had been hitherto subject."—*Contra Cels.* v. p. 398.

No. IV. (p. 57.)

THOUGH it may have appeared so to the men of that time under the guidance of their feelings; and though, in fact, *ancient* philosophers accompanied their denial of a Providence with the assertion, "that God contemplated himself only, because the contemplation of things external to himself involved a going out from himself and a dividing of the divine consciousness;" yet I will not say that such an *assertion*, taken in and by itself, must necessarily be accompanied with such a *denial*. The two erroneous propositions—"That God contemplates only himself, and no existences which are not himself," and, "That God must go out of himself in order to contemplate other beings, and, in order to care for them, must make use of the mediation of some other," were thus corrected through the medium of Christian teaching: "God's consciousness, however, is not, like man's, a faculty given to him, and of which, as being distinct from his original being, he has come into possession. But at one and the same moment (to speak after the manner of men) he emphatically *is*, and establishes himself as God; and, being thus established, he orders all other beings which exist only by virtue of his appointment."*

But man, on the contrary, starting from the position in which he finds himself, transfers to the Deity his notions of being and consciousness, and, still farther, of internal and external consciousness (which constitute the narrow sphere to which man's operations are confined). The consequence is, that he falls either into the lesser

* Ἐν ἀρχῇ ἦν ὁ λόγος, καὶ ὁ λόγος ἦν πρὸς τὸν θεὸν καὶ θεὸς ἦν ὁ λόγος πάντα δὶ αὐτοῦ ἐγένετο.

danger of a positive, or the greater danger of a negative, abstract anthropomorphism, while he virtually denies the existence of a Providence.

No. V. (p. 61.)

THE new direction of Christian philosophy here touched upon, showed itself most strikingly in Augustin. He thus expresses himself:* "The error of the old philosophers (who thought that they could not admit the idea of an original creation, but only a course of still repeated periods in which the Universe revolved, for fear of attributing any temporal variation to the understanding and will of God), originated in their attempt to measure by their *human, variable* and *limited* understanding, the completely *unchangeable*, and in every respect *infinite* understanding of God, who can number the *innumerable* without the process of a *change* of thought. They form a conception not of God (whom they are not able to conceive), but of themselves instead; they compare not *him* with *himself*, but *themselves* with *themselves*. When however He is *at first* said to be in a state of repose and then *afterwards* in a state of operation (though I, for my part, know not how this can be understood by *men*, inasmuch as, according to their present powers of conception, *they* can think of nothing new without experiencing a corresponding change), this *first* and *afterwards* doubtless was not in *Him*, but in the things which were called by Him out of nothing into being."

No. VI. (p. 62.)

THE idea of a necessarily existing, natural principle, external to the Deity, a principle from whose influence the necessity of evil in this lower world originated,—this idea of the antagonism of two worlds, was more closely connected with polytheism than might appear at first sight. It seemed necessary to fill up the interval between the two opposite degrees of existence, the highest degree, *viz.* the being of the Godhead, and the lowest, or natural existence; as the liberty of beings in the world of mortals was found to be limited, a higher world of beings was necessarily imagined, a world

* *De Civ. Dei*, xii. 17.

to which no evil can gain admission, because it is exalted above the *natural* principle.

Polytheism did not actually consist in a denial of the Divine Unity ; for the notion of this Unity is necessary to the mind of man, and inseparable from it. Indeed, it always lay at the foundation of all polytheistic religions, though more or less obscurely, and reflecting men have ever arrived at a consciousness of it. Polytheism consisted much more in the facts, that this unity was not felt to be present in actual life nor applied to the various relations of society; that men did not endeavor to raise themselves, their minds and hearts, *immediately* to the Supreme Godhead, but imagined, between it and themselves, a series of beings emanating, after their nature, from the Godhead, and not, like man (who thus directed his regard to them), exposed to the danger of falling.

The idea, therefore, of a God, must have been completely interwoven with the existence of a nation; and when monotheism became the prevailing belief, as among the Jews, there must necessarily arise a visible theocracy, founded thereupon ; nor could that notion ever become general among all the races of mankind except by the establishment of an invisible theocracy through the agency of Christianity. Now the great fact on which such a theocracy was founded was the Incarnation of God in the Person of his Son. Men now caught at the idea of a Mediator between God and themselves, one who partook of their own nature, who redeemed them from the dominion of evil and made them free ; they looked upon the Son of God as God himself, as him who held them in connection with God ; and the Spirit of God, God himself, as the source of power to hold communion with God.

A Constantine, a Chlodwig,* and, generally speaking, the uncivilized heathen nations which passed over to Christianity, conceived at first that they were but placing themselves under the care of a mightier God, the God of the Christians, who, when they had in vain cried to their former deities, had granted them help in war and protected them in time of danger. Prolix, philosophical demonstrations of the unity of the Godhead might well have produced no effect upon them; but when they had become accustomed,

* "Chlodwig" is the same as Cledovix, usually called *Clovis*.—*T.*

through the teaching of the Christian Church, to think of one only God in all the relations of life, polytheism of its own accord gradually disappeared.

Plotinus, in answer to the Gnostics, says (*Ep.* ii.), " Man should not only strive after the chief good, but also believe that there exists above him a series of perfect beings, ascending in a gradual succession up to the first source of Divine Existence ;"—the Christians, in fact, who rejected this notion, must have appeared to the polytheists as arrogant and egotistical. Plotinus acknowledged one First Cause of all being, *βασιλεῦς τῶν παντῶν, περὶ ὃν πάντα ἐστί*, yet he adds, that the greatness of this very Deity is shown most of all in the number of the gods ; " He cannot know the power of God who would contract the Divinity into *one*, but he who exhibits it in its multifarious revelation, so that God, himself remaining the same, produces many others, all of whom are conformed to his will, existing through him and by him." We may compare with this what the same writer says in the same treatise, of the necessarily confined powers of the human soul in relation to the free Spirit of God, as it reveals itself in the regular course of the heavens, by way of illustration and voucher for what has been said above : " There can be none of those things *there* which make men vile *here;* there is no wretched body clogging and retarding the soul." (*Ibid.* p. 206.)

With that distinction of two worlds, and with the assumption of a necessarily existing, natural principle, descending from the Godhead to the lowest scale of being, was connected also a distinction between man and man in respect to their relation to the Deity. " Among them also (says Plotinus, in the treatise we have already quoted) there must necessarily be a graduated scale ; for the life of men is of a twofold character, that of the best among them and that of the great mass, the former alone being directed to the supreme good ; and again, the mode of life is twofold in the *human being*, in those who have a regard for virtue and obtain a portion of that good, and, on the other hand, in the vulgar herd who, as laborers and handicraftsmen, minister to the wants of the higher and nobler class." It was only through the teaching of " God manifest in the flesh," and of the redemption wrought by Him, that this line of demarkation was removed, and a common way to the highest happiness, a communion with God even in this life, was opened to all men alike, without distinction.

This opposition of Christianity to the existing tone of thought, whether philosophical, moral, or religious, displayed itself especially in the different sects which arose in the Christian Church of the first centuries; since they were nothing but attempts made to accommodate Christianity to the various modes of human thought, and even to amalgamate it with them. Their attack, therefore, fell chiefly on its characteristic and distinguishing doctrines; for instance, the creation and the connection of the world with God as its Creator; the redemption; the incarnation of the Son of God "in the form of a servant;" a universal belief adequate to the wants of all mankind; morality as the basis of religion, and the close connection of practice with theory.

In the first heresies in relation to the doctrine of the creation, there was a fluctuation between pantheism, dualism, and the attempt to deduce the duality from the unity *through the assumption of an accident.** Hermogenes took the idea from the ἄπειρον, a natural principle on which the creation was grounded, the raw material which, though perfectly undefined in itself, was organized by the power of the Deity, and from which the defects in the creation originated; he sought to avoid the anthropomorphic representation, "that God then first begun to form this matter," by teaching "that these two principles (God's plastic power and boundless matter) differing according to their respective natures, operated the one upon the other by their mere existence, without any commencement *in time.*" "God in making use of that inorganic matter did not in the full sense of the word create the world, but only in appearance and by an approximation of himself towards it; like the impression which beauty makes by its mere appearance, or like the effect produced by the magnet by merely approaching an object."†

Philosophy, without giving any strict explanation of its origin, was yet driven to the task of bringing this ἄπειρον (on which the older philosophers had supported themselves) to some sort of agreement with the improved system, and to form deductions therefrom. From this attempt proceeded the view to which such an explanation must necessarily lead the human understanding; *viz.*, that in the successive gradations of being, developing itself from its highest

* In the German—"durch die Annahme *eines Falls.*"—*T.*

† See Tertullian, *Opp.* p. 355.

source, this pure limitation and negation of being was the last; because after it there could follow no other existence. And, secondly, that this limitation and negation (the ἄπειρον) was evil itself in the abstract, and became the cause of all defect or evil in the lower departments of creation.

The Gnostics, on the contrary, did not consider natural evil as something necessary and self-existing, but deduced the beginning of the actual creation from a withdrawal (*entfurnung*) of the Supreme; and therefore they came into collision with the former system, that of Plotinus. According to the poetico-philosophical system of Valentinus, one of the profoundest of them, "there arose among the spirits that had emanated from God a desire to search into the nature of the incomprehensible, eternal Father, and to penetrate, beyond the limits of their individual existence, into his being and essence. Now when these emanations aspire beyond their individuality, they are in danger of destroying themselves; and from this idle attempt to oppose the law of nature is produced an unsubstantial monstrosity, fluctuating between existence and non-existence, the first analogon to matter. This irregular being had spread its influence from the highest to the lowest order of emanations or *Eons;* but in each of them this rebellious movement was afterwards *subdued* through the power of the redemption, though it had eventually acquired too great strength to be altogether *annihilated;* and therefore the lower, visible world, was formed out of these same emanations.* Some followers of Valentinus endeavored to find a still higher link, from which the chain of emanations proceeded; they pretended to explain the origin of the inscrutable being (Βύθος) which possessed the exercise of self-consciousness, for they conceded to it ἐννοία, or the understanding of its own thoughts; and they considered that the Supreme of all was probably an unconscious, unthinking original.† Epiphanes of Alexandria seems to have carried out, in his teaching, the pantheistic system to the greatest lengths; for, *antecedently to all intelligent beings,* he maintained that there was, as the first source of existence, an Incomprehensible Unity‡ (eine unbegreifliche Einheit),

* Compare the *mythic* part of the account as it is given in Irenæus, with the *philosophical* in Origen.—*Dial. c. Marcion.* Sect. iv.

† Προαρχὴ ἀνεννόητος.

‡ Μονότης προανεννόητος ἀῤῥητος και ἀνονόμαστος.

from whence proceeded the self-conscious Unity (die sich ihrer selbst bewusste Einheit), and, through that, all other beings.*

The pantheistic principle displayed itself also in the injurious effect upon morals produced by the practical working of its doctrines. It considered all moral and civil laws as destructive of that community and union for which all nature is striving; it accounted all *property*, all claims whatever to individual appropriation, to be an unnatural limitation; that until man could elevate himself to a due sense of that Supreme Unity, he must remain subject to the individual forms to which the creation is confined, and must still run through all those forms, returning again and again into life under different appearances, until he has raised himself to a dominion over those forms and to the knowledge of the Supreme Unity, and so, at length, be permitted to return thereto. The soul of Christ was asserted to have been distinguished only by its retaining a clearer remembrance of that One Supreme, and therefore by a dominion over all the various forms of the creation and over its laws (for thus, probably, were his miracles accounted for); and every other soul also, by following him, might raise itself to the same dignity; but through faith and love only can man attain to the highest happiness, all other individual actions being, in and by themselves, neither good nor bad.†

No. VII. (p. 64.)

THIS idea of the exalted dignity of every thing human, and of the honor paid to the Godhead "in the form of a servant," showed itself also in the rites of Christian worship as it departed more from its

* Clemens Alexand. therefore calls him the author of the γνῶσις μοναστίκη.

† Compare Irenæus, i. 3, and 26. Clemens Alex. *Stromata.* Traces of a pantheistic view of mythology among the Greeks (according to which the histories of their gods were looked upon as merely allegorical representations of the metamorphoses of the universe) are met with in Plutarch, *de* 'Ει *apud Delph.* c. 9. Irenæus, here referred to (ii. 4), calls Valentinus the Gnostic "worse than a pagan." After a formal discussion of gnostic speculations, "concludit mundi opificium soli Deo ascribendum esse," and asserts that their "Pleroma, Bythus, Sige, et Vacuum —una cum professoribus *vacua* esse et *inania*."—*T.*

original simplicity. The enthusiastic defenders of image worship felt this; and it was this feeling which gave them an assurance that in their adoration of saints and relics they were not falling into the sin of idolatry. This feeling was expressed very strongly in the answer of John of Damascus to the objection raised upon the prohibition of image-worship in the commandments given to the Jews. "It is true," he says, "that the Israelites of old built no temple dedicated to any name of man; they solemnized no festivals in memory of departed men; since man's nature was still under the curse, death was still a sentence of condemnation; the dead body, and whosoever touched it, were looked upon as unclean. But now, since the Godhead has been united with our nature as a quickening means of grace, that nature has been ennobled and raised to an imperishable condition. Therefore the death of the saints is commemorated as a festival, temples have been built in honor of their names, and images designed to represent them. Formerly the temples were adorned with forms and figures of irrational creatures, but now with the images of saints who made themselves, by their holy life, true and living temples of God who dwelt within them." *Orat.* ii.

No. VIII. (p. 65.)

The feeling with which both philosophers and rulers regarded Christianity, was influenced by the extension which that eclecticism obtained. Some who sought for traces of divinity in all religions, without distinction, looked upon Christianity also as a sort of theosophy, though they censured the intolerance of Christians with regard to all other religions. Thus, to take an instance, Amelius, a philosopher of the New Platonic school, quoted the first words of St. John's Gospel, and understood by the Λόγος, the creating Spirit that mediates between things temporal and eternal, between essential being and derived.* So, also, the emperor Heliogabalus was led, by this prevailing idea, to form a plan for making the worship of his *Syrian Deity* the dominant religion for the whole world, while he placed all other religions in connection therewith, and wished to bring them over to it by degrees, as so many different forms of the same. He therefore called all other deities servants of this god,

* Euseb. *Præp. Evang.* xi. 19.

and intended to transplant the Mysteries and holy vessels of all religions (including the sacred things of Jews and Christians) to his temple at Rome, and to make his priests supreme directors of the universal religion.*

The respect felt by the emperor Alexander Severus for Christianity, proceeded from a similar view. It is well known that he had in his palace two places set apart for sacred uses, in one of which (where he worshipped as soon as he rose in the morning) were the busts of "really divine men," as Abraham and Orpheus, of Christ also, and of Alexander the Great; in the other the busts of those who, though great, "yet remained within the bounds of human nature"—as Virgil, Cicero, Achilles.† On the occasion of a dispute for the possession of a public place between the Christians and the purveyors of dressed meat, he decided that it was better that the Deity should, at least, after some fashion, be always honored there, than that it should be appropriated to cooks' shops.‡ He therefore also formed a plan of erecting a temple to Christ, and to have his name enrolled amongst the gods.

The emperor Constantine also is known to have advanced by degrees from honoring Christianity as one of the best forms of religion, and Christ as one of the mightiest Gods, to a full conviction that Christianity was the only true religion, and that it alone should be the established worship in his empire. Sopatros, a supporter of the ancient religion and of the Platonic philosophy, lived in familiar intercourse with him,§ which may account for the view he at first took of the doctrinal disputes of Christians. When he had relinquished the polytheistic view of religion, it might still appear to him a matter of indifference how men defined the relation in which Christ stood to the Deity. He wrote thus to Alexander, bishop of Alexandria, as well as to Arius:—"Such inquiries as were not dictated by *necessity* nor prescribed by any *divine precept*, but were occasioned only by an idle and unprofitable spirit of disputation, must not lightly be exhibited before their *public* assemblies, even if they were engaged in as an exercise of intellectual ability." Again, he

* See Æl. Lampid. *Vit. Heliogab.*, ch. 3 and 7.

† *Ibid.* ch 29 and 31.

‡ *Vit. Heliogab.* ch. 49.

§ See Eunap. *Vit. Ædes.*

spoke of the *weakness* of *human* nature which was unable to explain such things, and he referred to the example of the philosophers, all of whom (agreeably to the eclecticism of that day) held one doctrine in common with each other, though they were far removed from one another on *individual points*. "How much more then were the servants of the *Most High God* bound to agree together in their religious opinions of that great God, who, as the common Redeemer of all, had given to all a common source of light." Since all men cannot have the same inclinations, the same disposition, the same opinions, he thought it enough if they only agree in one faith in the Divine Providence. His plan was, not only to unite the whole empire under one sceptre, but also to connect all his subjects together through one religion; and this, "because it would tend most to the good of his empire, if all the worshippers of God agreed with each other in their mode of worshipping him." He probably believed that Christianity was the best adapted for such a purpose, as containing all the best features of all other religious systems.*

With this same view (which indeed prevailed even in the fifth century) the philosopher Themistius, though not a Christian, could live on intimate terms with the Christian emperors, as well as with the emperor Julian. He maintained also a friendly intercourse with the Christian theologians (especially those of the school of Origen) who promoted the study of ancient literature. He exhorted Julian, on his accession to the throne, since he was raised by the Deity to the same station where Hercules and Bacchus once stood, to be at once philosopher and governor, and to purify the world from the evil with which it was deluged.† He endeavored to persuade the Christian emperors of his time to exercise a tolerant forbearance towards all religious parties. He praised the emperor Jovian for his toleration, in a manner which shows his active efforts to withdraw him from intolerance of all kinds. "God," he says, "has implanted in the nature of all men a talent or capacity for religion, but has left the manner of worshipping him to the will of each individual. The differences in religious worship and their contending claims, contributed very greatly (according to the plan of Providence) to keep alive amongst men a constant reverence for God. All religions had

* *Ep. Constantin. ap. Euseb. Vit. Constant.* ii. 64, et seq.

† *Ep. Themist. ad Julian.* p. 254. Julian. *Opp.* Ed. Spanh.

but one *object*, but the *way* that led to it was different in each, and, according to the constitution of *human nature*, it must necessarily be so." (Themist. *Orat.* v.) By similar arguments, brought forward with all the ardor of conviction, he tried to appease the fury with which the emperor Valens, as an Arian, persecuted the party of Athanasius.*

This turn of mind on religious matters was displayed also by the historian Marcellinus,† who endeavored to find something divine in all religions, and paid respect to the doctrines of Christianity and to those Christian priests who fulfilled its requirements. He considered, in this view, the controversies of Christians to be the corruption of Christianity. He said of Constantine, "that he had mixed the perfect and simple character of Christianity with weak and effeminate superstitions, and had stirred up many controversies which arose from subtle speculations, foreign from the dignity that became that religion.‡

Others, indeed, were not so fair-dealing towards Christianity; partly because they attributed a divine origin to that form of religion alone which had been handed down to the nations from olden time, and because they were embittered against Christ's religion by the previous oppression which Polytheism had undergone; partly from reasons already mentioned; as, for instance, Libanius, and others of the New-Platonic school. Evidences of that religious eclecticism in the age of Augustine are to be found in his Epistles.§ "We invoke," he says in his last Epistle, "the power of God, distributed through the works of creation, under *many* different names, because his *proper* name is unknown to us all." It is interesting to follow in the development of Augustine's character his transition from Platonic eclecticism to the catholic Christian Church. At a later period‖ he stated his view of the Greek philosophy, of which we give a concise abstract here, for the sake of the truth on which it is founded: "Whilst seeking for the 'highest good' in aught else than God, man could not but fall into the error of looking for it either in what affects his body or in the faculties of his soul; and whilst he

* See Socrates, *Ecc. Hist.* iv. 32.

† A cotemporary of Julian.—*T.*

‡ Socrat. xxi. 16.

§ Augustin. *Epist.* 21 and 43.

‖ *Epist.* 56.

acknowledged such a chief good, he could neither discover the actual rule of truth that extends over soul and body, nor yet the true source of all things. The two most celebrated forms in which this error was exhibited, were those of the Epicureans and the Stoics. The Platonists, on the other hand, had discovered in the Divine Wisdom the source of all happiness and of every true good, as well as the origin of all being, and the only unerring standard of truth; since, however, they were not able to master the true doctrine of man's sensual nature on the one side, nor the vain egotism of human reason on the other, they contented themselves at first with combating these different and opposite semblances of the truth, and adopted the dry husk of skepticism. Both these species of error, therefore, opposed themselves to the preaching of St. Paul at Athens. But when the truth, as it is displayed with divine power in Christianity, became known, those errors at length disappeared, and Platonism, laying aside the empty shell, and venturing again to appear in its pure form, became, and continues to be, the only philosophy in connection with Christianity."

No. IX. (p. 72.)

I INTRODUCE here the allegorical narrative in which Julian describes his own history and fortunes.*—" A certain rich man (Constantine) who had partly inherited from his father, and partly acquired great riches, by right or wrong (for he paid little regard to the gods), divided this vast wealth among his sons, on whose education he had bestowed no care, from an idea that riches were all in all for them. Now as one of these sons wished to possess the whole of the property, there soon arose among them scenes of murder and sad confusion. The ancient shrines of their forefathers, which the father had already treated with contempt, were now thrown down by the sons, and robbed of the gifts which their ancestors had dedicated.

"On the site of the destroyed temples modern *tombs*† were erected, since fortune (Τύχη) had forewarned them that, as they had despised the gods, they would soon require *many sepulchres*.

* See his 7th Oration.

† That is, chapels built over the graves of the martyrs.

When, therefore, every thing divine and human was thus outraged, Jupiter was moved by the state of things, and looking to the god of the sun (Helios), he said, 'Wilt thou still forbear to take vengeance upon this proud and insolent man, who by deserting thy worship hath brought himself and all his family into such an unhappy state? Or dost thou think, because thou dischargest not thine arrows against his race, that therefore thou art the less to be blamed for this misfortune? for this house is *abandoned* by thee.'—The fates were then obliged, in compliance with the will of Jove, to spin a new thread of life;* and again he addressed Helios, 'Behold this child; he is nearly related to those sons, but has been thrown aside into a corner and despised. He is nephew to that rich man, and cousin to his heirs; henceforth he is thy son. Swear to me, therefore, by my sceptre and thine own, that he shall be thy special care, that thou wilt watch over him, and wilt heal his present sickness; for thou seest how the child is covered with soot and dirt,† and what danger there is that the fire implanted in him by thee should go out. Take him therefore to thyself, and educate him.'—Helios rejoiced when he heard this of the boy, in whom he saw a faint spark of his own immortal nature still remaining; and from that time he took charge of his education, and bore him away from scenes of bloodshed and the din of battle. Jupiter also commanded Minerva (born without mother and ever-virgin goddess) to educate the boy in conjunction with Helios.

"When now the youth was grown up, and looked back upon the mass of evil which had befallen him from the hands of his own kinsmen and cousins, he was so astounded at its amount that he resolved to throw himself down to Tartarus. Helios, however, so benevolently inclined towards him, and Minerva (who watches over men), lulled him into a deep sleep, and drew him off from these thoughts. On again awaking, he went into a solitary place, and then, resting for a while upon a stone which he found there, he reflected by himself how he could escape from such overwhelming evils, unrelieved by the appearance of a single good. Upon this Mercury (who was indeed of a kindred nature with him) appeared

* For Julian himself.

† An implied insult, probably, to the rites and doctrines of Christianity in which Julian was educated.—*T.*

to him in the form of a young man, greeted him in a friendly manner, and spoke thus: 'Come hither, and I will guide thee to a level path, if thou canst but surmount this short space of rough and steep ground where thou seest all others stumbling and at length turning back.'

"The youth followed him thither with much circumspection, carrying with him a sword, a shield, and a dart; but his head was still uncovered, and he came to a smooth untrodden path full of fruits and flowers. Mercury, upon that, led him to a large and lofty mountain, and said, 'On the summit of this mountain is seated the father of the gods; take heed then (for there is great danger even here) that thou worship him with reverent devotion, and ask ever of him what thou wishest for; let thy wish however and thy choice, my son, be that which is not only good, but *the best*. Mercury having thus spoken, disappeared; the young man, wishing to ask his advice as to what he should pray for to the father of the gods, but seeing him no more, reflected within himself that the counsel already given, though not complete, was yet good. 'I will, therefore (said he to himself), at once pray for that which is *best* for me, even though I see not clearly the father of the gods. O father Jupiter (he continued), or under whatever name thou art best pleased to be invoked, show me the way that leadeth up to thee; for that bright region which surroundeth thee (if I may judge from the charms of that to which we have ascended) seemeth far too beautiful to confine thy splendor.'

"As he thus prayed he fell into a sleep, or trance; and he beheld Helios himself, the invisible god, of whom the sun in the heavens is the visible symbol. Beside himself at this sight, the young man spoke thus, 'To thee, O father of the gods, I henceforth entirely devote myself, in gratitude for all this which thou hast shown me.' Clinging with his hands to the knees of Helios, he besought him to take him into his protection. The god on this summoned Minerva before him: but first of all he asked to see the weapons he had brought with him; and, observing that he had only a sword, a shield, and a javelin, 'Where then, my son, is your gorgoneum and your helmet?' 'Even these (he answered) have I obtained with much difficulty and exertion; for no one took part with me, who lay neglected and despised in the house of my kinsmen.'

'What then (said the great god Helios) sayest thou to the necessity which is laid upon thee of returning, at all hazards, to that house again?' Then the young man begged that he would not send him back thither, but rather keep him with him, lest he might never again return to him, but sink under the evils that awaited him there. As he persisted still in asking this, even with tears, Helios said to him, 'Thou art yet young and unconsecrated; come then to us that thou mayest receive consecration. Then shalt thou abide there in safety, for there thou must necessarily abide to expiate all those godless doings; but remember, thou canst call me and Minerva and the other gods to your aid.'

"The young man on hearing this stood in silence; at length the great god Helios led him to an eminence which was full of light towards the top, but at the foot of it was spread a sheer mist, through which, as well as on the adjoining water, the light and splendor of Helios only dimly penetrated. 'Seest thou,' he asked, 'thy cousin, the heir to the property?' and he said, 'I see him.'—'And seest thou also these herdsmen? What doth the heir appear now to be doing? and what the herdsmen?'—The young man answered, 'He sleepeth much, and giveth himself up secretly to a life of pleasure; among the herdsmen are some well conducted and attentive to their duty, but most of them are rude and worthless, who consume and sell the herds, and injure their master doubly; since they so ruin the herds that they can only expect from him moderate wages, and then they murmur and complain of him; as if it would not be better to earn their full and complete wages, than thus to injure the herd intrusted to them.' 'What now,' added the god, 'if I, together with Minerva, at the suggestion of Jupiter, should make thee ruler over all instead of this heir?' On this the youth again resisted, and begged permission to remain where he was. But Helios said, 'Be not disobedient, lest I become as indignant and displeased with thee as I now love and esteem thee.'

"On this he answered, 'O great Helios, and I call Minerva and Jove himself also to witness, do with me what ye will.' Mercury then, again becoming visible to the youth, inspired him with courage, since he felt that he had now recovered his former guide. 'Receive then,' said Minerva, 'these kindly meant admonitions. Observe that this heir takes no pleasure in the *best* of his herdsmen; but the bad ones, and those who take the trouble to flatter him, have succeeded in making him their slave. This is the cause that he is not loved by the good servants, while he suffers much wrong from these pretended friends. Take thou then especial heed, that when thou art come into possession, thou prefer not the flatterer to the true friend. Listen also, my son, to this, my second suggestion ; that voluptuary yonder, who spends the greater part of his time in sleep, is generally cheated and imposed upon; be thou, therefore, sober and vigilant, that the flatterer deceive thee not under the show of candor. Hearken to yet a third piece of advice: take good heed to thyself, and yield not to a shy excess of modesty, except before us and those of men who are like us; for you cannot but see how injurious a false shame has proved to him.'

" Helios then took up the discourse, and said: 'The friends whom thou choosest, treat as friends; view them not as slaves or servants, since you perceive how distrust of his friends hath plunged this man into ruin. Love those who are subject to thee as we love thee. Extend to every good man the friendship which thou sharest with us, for we are indeed thy benefactors, friends, and protectors.'

" At hearing this the young man cheered up, and professed himself ready to obey the gods in all things. 'Come on then,' said Helios to him, 'only take good courage, since we will every where be with thee: I and Minerva and Mercury, nay, along with us, all the gods who are in Olympus, in the air, or on the earth; in short, the whole family of the gods. Therefore be devout towards us, true to thy friends, affectionate to thy dependents; and, while thou exercisest thy authority over them for their improvement, be neither a slave to thine own desires nor yet to theirs.

" 'In addition to the armor thou broughtest with thee, receive this torch from me, that its strong light may illuminate thee on earth, and that thou mayest not miss the light which thou hast enjoyed here. Take also the gorgoneum and helmet of Minerva, and Mercury will give thee his golden wand. Furnished with such armor, go travel over every land and every sea, fearlessly obeying our laws. Nor let any one *there* induce thee to forget these our admonitions; for by following them thou wilt be at once beloved and honored by us, respected by all our faithful servants, and feared by all wicked men. Know then that thy *body* was given thee for this sole purpose, that by thy means, out of our regard to thy fathers, we may purify their house. Therefore remember that thou hast an immortal *soul*, which is descended from us; so that, at length, by imitating our example thou mayest thyself become a god, and with us ever behold the face of our father.' "

No. X. (p. 74.)

JULIAN himself, in his Epistle to the Athenians, says that he spent six years at that place with his brother Gallus, until the latter was called to the imperial court; this then was about A. D. 350.* Sozomen, *loco citato*, expressly speaks of his departure thence for Constantinople, and from thence to Nicomedia, in this order. Socrates makes him go in the first instance from Constantinople to Nicomedia, entirely omitting the intervening period of his residence in Cappadocia; and therefore he mixes up together his first and his second sojourn at Constantinople.

So also does Libanius; and what he says, in his panegyric of Julian, that he (Libanius) began to teach in Constantinople at the same time when Julian began to study philosophy, applies to his first residence there. On the other hand, what he says† of the curiosity and attention which Julian excited, and the consequent uneasiness of the emperor, belongs only to the second.

No. XI. (p. 77.)

JULIAN according to his own declaration (in his *Ep.* li. *ad Alex.*) was a sincere Christian up to his twentieth year. This coincides with the year 351, in which he came to Nicomedia. According to Libanius (see his *Panegyric*) he actually hated the gods, until the prophecies which he met with there produced a change in his opinions. Indeed, Augustine* says that a Greek oracular response was extant in his time, to this effect: " Peter by magic arts hath caused that Christ should be worshipped for three hundred and sixty-five years; but after the lapse of that time Christianity shall cease to exist."

* Compare Sozom. v. 2, Gregor. Naz. *Orat.* i. *Stelit.*, and Ammian. Marcellin. xv. 2.

† In his treatise, *In necem Juliani*.

* *De Civit. Dei*, xviii. 53.

The same Libanius, in his oration on Julian's death, says that the discourse of a philosopher of the New Platonic school wrought this conversion. We may combine together the two statements of Socrates and Sozomen. As to what Gregory Nazianzen relates (*Orat.* i. *Stelit.*), 'that he had already expressed his aversion to Christianity to his brother, by constantly defending the cause of the ancient religion in his rhetorical exercises with him, under the pretext of "making the worse appear the better cause,"*—it is not at all probable, since during his residence in Cappadocia, where alone he could have held these disputations, he was still a sincere Christian.

Nor does the account of Ammianus (xxii. 9), "that the well-known Eusebius, Bishop of Nicomedia, was Julian's instructor during his residence in that city," quite agree with chronological dates; since Eusebius was appointed Bishop of Constantinople before the Synod of Antioch, A. D. 341, at which he was present in that character, and died soon after.†

No. XII. (p. 79.)

According to Eunapius (in his *Life of Maximus*), Julian became acquainted with Maximus subsequent to his intercourse with Chrysanthius. The account, as given by Eunapius, is intrinsically not improbable; it is at least characteristic of that period: "The philosopher Eusebius, who was much with Chrysanthius, was wont to conclude his philosophical investigations with the remark, 'This is the truth as it really exists; magical operations, on the contrary, only deceive the senses, and are performed by sorcerers who have suffered themselves to be carried away by the discovery and application of certain powers and properties of matter.'"

Eager to learn the proper application of such language, Julian was at length told by Eusebius, that they referred to Maximus, who imagined that the *greatness* of his natural endowments allowed him to despise the ordinary *way of demonstration!* "You need not, however," added the philosopher, "be astonished at this, but rather by elevating your powers of reason above the delusions of mere

* τὸν ἥττω λόγον κρείττω ποίειν, "To make the worse appear the better cause."

† See Sozom. iii. 4 and 7.

sense, look upon such operations *upon the senses* as really implying nothing great." Julian, however, immediately took leave of him, with the striking words—" *You may stay here with your books*, but you have described to me the very man I am seeking for;" and so saying, he hastened to Ephesus in search of Maximus.

But, according to Sozomen* (who is the most accurate writer concerning the life of Julian), the great change in Julian's opinions was at the first completely wrought by the instructions and the prophecies of Maximus at Nicomedia, who had been induced by the reputation of Julian to go thither. And indeed it quite agrees with the character of Maximus, that he should first have conceived the idea of gaining over so promising a youth of the imperial family to his religion, and with the fact of his having made a collection of oracular predictions. To this may be added, that Julian himself calls him his instructor in the study of the ancient poets, which, after the symbolic method of exposition then prevalent, was combined with the study of philosophy and theosophy; a method which most readily afforded opportunities of refuting the charges brought by the Christians against heathenism, and of recommending the latter under the most favorable aspects.†

The Oration above referred to, was delivered by Julian‡ during his expedition against the Persians. It was Maximus who (according to the testimony of Eunapius himself, and also on the authority of an Epistle addressed to him) was invited to court at the very beginning of his reign, and remained constantly with him to his death.§ It is probable therefore that by the expression (in note *) " the philosopher here present," Maximus is to be understood: since in the speech addressed to the emperor by Libanius|| *Nicocles* is spoken of as one not present. The description¶ however of " the *absent* follower, who, after the preparatory instructions of Maximus,

* And also according to Socrates.

† *Orat.* vii. p. 235; and he speaks of him as *actually present*—Τουτοῦι τοῦ φιλοσόφου.

‡ According to Libanius, in *Julian. nec.* p. 300. Part II. ed. Paris.

§ See Ammian. xxv. 3.

|| In the *Legat. ad Julian.*

¶ Julian *loc. cit.*

had initiated Julian in the mysteries of philosophy, agrees altogether with what we know of Chrysanthius. While Maximus enjoyed greatly the splendor of the palace and the respect which was paid him by the emperor, Chrysanthius, on the contrary, steadily refused to come to court, notwithstanding Julian's frequent invitations.

Some well-grounded passages of history, the well-known characters of Chrysanthius, Maximus, and Julian himself, and the influence exercised over the latter by Maximus, may have given occasion for the getting up of this account.

Does not the language* of Libanius tend to prove that Maximus produced the change of religion in Julian by his philosophical instructions at Nicomedia; and that in order to confirm him in that change, he took him from Nicomedia, where he was too closely surrounded and watched by the Christians, to go with him into Ionia? "I bless that day," he says, "as the commencement of the world's freedom, and that place (Nicomedia) where this change was brought about, and that physician of his soul, who, when the profession of heathenism was forbidden by the laws, nobly exposed himself to the greatest danger of that period, and sailed safely with his pupil through the Cyanean rocks."†

Julian himself‡ speaks of the dangers and sufferings which threatened him on the part of his relations and friends, when he first on his journey to Ionia went over to the Hellenic religion.

No. XIII. (p. 106.)

Julian found the philosophic doctrine of the relation of the natural to the divine (of nature to the Deity) in the myth of Cybele and Atys; how through one efficient, energizing power, extending from the Supreme to the last of the gods (who is placed next in order before *material* forms) even to the limits of all existence, the whole is formed and kept in perpetual order. Cybele, accordingly, is the second in the rank of Deity; from the highest or Supreme Deity (the source of all being, stretching out beyond and over all individual existence), she receives full and complete life and energizing power. She thereby produces life of the second degree, *i. e.*

* See his *Panegyr. in Jul. cons.* † *Ibid.* p. 234.
‡ *Epist. ad Themist.* p. 259.

the casuative (or creative), spiritual (or immaterial) gods. Of these Atys, the last produced, (who receives in his own person the energizing power of all the rest, and extends it to the material beings over whose formation he presides,) remains united through her with the one Supreme. In proportion however as he turns away from her to the plurality of existences over which he is placed, he loses his connection with the Supreme Unity, and is carried away by the endless attractions of matter. This process goes on till Providence again draws him back to the unity, while she gives figure and shape to matter throughout its appointed organized forms. (The emasculation of Atys seems to point to this.) The return of Atys to the Supreme Unity was indicated by the sounding trumpets of the Corybantes.

The moral application of this myth to men consists in this: that the gods admonish us, even in our inner man, to restrain all capricious disregard of law and order, to subdue that inner man by means of the higher law, and to bring it back to that law, and, if possible, to the One Supreme himself. Then Julian speaks (p. 171) of the festival of expiation, called *Hilaria*;* "Nevertheless the order of things was at no time different from what it is now. Atys is still subject to his mother, is still working out a succession of existences in the world, and is still forming within himself the indefinite and endless by means of ideal forms definite in themselves."

In the text of the Spanheim edition of Julian, and of the subjoined translation, the sense here is altogether mistaken. According to that version, Julian is made desirous of showing the similarity of the birth of Bacchus with that of Hercules. This, however, is quite contrary to his meaning; since his object is to refute those who maintain that the former of these gods was, like the latter, raised from the human to the divine nature in consideration of his godlike services. With this view he places the two narratives by the side of each other, and shows that Hercules, amidst his extraordinary powers, yet exhibits always a likeness to human nature, but that this likeness is not to be found in the character of Bacchus. He then observes, that this distinction should preserve men from the danger of looking upon Bacchus as a deified mortal rather than a real and true

* This festival was celebrated at Rome, in connection with the worship of Cybele, at the vernal equinox. See Ovid's *Fasti*. iv. 337.—*T.*

god. The passage therefore, in p. 219, instead of ὅπου γὰρ ἡ γένεσις ἐστὶν, should be οὐ γὰρ, κ.τ.λ., and should be translated "neque enim talis generatio Bacchi est, qualis Herculis." And at p. 220, instead of κατά τ.ι τοῖς ἀνθρώποις προσέοικεν, it should be interrogatively, κατά τι, κ.τ.λ; and translated—"humanarum rerum simile quid num continet?"

No. XIV. (p. 108.)

At a later period (that of the disputes about image worship) the same reasons were adduced in defence of the practice, and that by deep-thinking men; for instance, that in the type man worships the archetype; that the sensual nature of man could not *immediately* be elevated to the notion of the Invisible, it therefore seeks to bring it *objectively* home to him by means of appropriate representations. We may compare with this a remarkable passage in Damascenus. "The apostles," he says, "beheld the Lord with their bodily eyes, as others saw the apostles and martyrs. I also long to see them with body and soul, since I am formed of a twofold nature; and I therefore pray to the Visible Image not as God, but as to a venerable representation of The Venerable. Thou, forsooth, more exalted and independent of sense than I am, despisest all sensible representation; but I, who am but a man, and have a human body, take a pleasure in thus associating with the saints after a sensible manner, and in thus seeing them with my bodily eyes." See Damasc. *Opp.* p. 717.

No. XV. (p. 113.)

The comparison of the Christians with this species of cynics seems to have suggested itself before Julian's time, and was commonly made; Lucian, accordingly, who has drawn the picture of such a cynic in the person of Peregrinus Proteus, speaks of them as finding a very favorable reception with the Christians.

No. XVI. (p. 115.)

Celsus asserted that the Barbarians certainly *find out* religious precepts, but the Greeks had the talent of examining the discoveries of the Barbarians, of fixing their value, and employing them in the service of virtue. To this Origen replied, "that the remark served admirably for the defence of Christianity; since any one who came with a mind rightly educated in Greek science to the study of Christian doctrines, would upon examination discover the truth thereof, apply them to the business of life, and also prove the truth of Christianity by means of a philosophical method, after the manner of the Greeks." See Origen *contr. Cels.* i. 2.

No. XVII. (p. 116.)

At the time of Origen, as he relates, veneration for the three patriarchs, Abraham, Isaac, and Jacob, was so general, that all magicians, both in their writings and in their conjurations, called upon the God of Abraham, Isaac, and Jacob, and ascribed especial power to this designation of the Deity.

No. XVIII. (p. 123.)

Lucian, in his Peregrinus Proteus, had already spoken of the active beneficence of the Christians towards all their brethren in the faith, as a means by which many persons had been induced to adopt it. Christianity certainly first took away the narrow distinctions which had existed between different nations and different classes.—The monasteries also were already, in the last half of the fourth century, the frequent means of promoting the union of the lower with the higher classes, and the spread of a more general education. Slaves, whom their masters, as a meritorious act, had set free, *there* came in contact with the rich and the distinguished who had retired thither; and there under careful superintendence they were gradually prepared for the free use of their natural powers, and the filling of a higher station.*

Julian also could not have denied that a venerable life distinguished the Christian clergy, even though he pronounced these venerable manners to be only a sort of hypocrisy.

An historical writer,† and certainly no partial witness in this re-

* See Augustin. *de Opere Monachor.*

† Ammianus Marcellinus, who wrote not long after the time of Julian.

spect, while describing the worldly life of the bishops of Rome, adds this remark: "It would indeed be happy for them if they lived after the pattern of some of the provincial bishops, who by their temperance, the poorness of their clothing, and their downcast eyes, recommend themselves as truly modest men, both to the God whom they serve and to their sincere followers and admirers."

THE END.